✝ *We Sing and Praise*

MUSIC SERIES FOR CATHOLIC SCHOOLS

We Sing and Chant

BY

SISTER CECILIA, S.C., M.F.A.

Supervisor of Music, *Sisters of Charity of Seton Hill*
Greensburg, Pennsylvania

SISTER JOHN JOSEPH, C.S.J., Ph.D.

Director of Department of Music, *Fontbonne College*
St. Louis, Missouri

SISTER ROSE MARGARET, C.S.J., M.M.

Supervisor of Music in Elementary Schools
Sisters of Saint Joseph of Carondelet, St. Louis, Missouri

Illustrations by BERYL JONES, MARTHA SETCHELL, *and* RUTH WOOD

Ginn and Company

Boston · New York · Chicago · Atlanta · Dallas · Palo Alto · Toronto

© COPYRIGHT, 1958, BY GINN AND COMPANY
PHILIPPINES COPYRIGHT, 1958, BY GINN AND COMPANY

No part of this book protected by the copyright hereon may be reproduced in any form without written permission of the publisher.

Acknowledgments

Acknowledgment is due to publishers, composers, and authors for permission to **reprint** songs and poems in this book, as follows:

D. Appleton Century Company, "Bye, Baby, Bye" (words only) by Eudora S. Bumstead; The Apostleship of Prayer, "Our Lady's Lullaby" by Sister M. Rose Alma Herbert, S.H.N., from the *Messenger of the Sacred Heart*; *Ave Maria*, words of "Christmas Blessings" by Katherine Edelman, words of "Bedtime" by L. Mitchell Thornton, words of "Old Man Thunder" and "Wind and Rain" by Helen Howland Prommel, words of "Prayer for a Little Child" by Josephine Moroney; Bruce Publishing Company, words of "Saint Joseph's Song" by Rev. Gerald Fitzgerald, C.S.C., from *A Lovely Gate Set Wide*, compiled by Sister Margaret Patrice; *Children's Activities*, "A Valentine Surprise" (words only) by Alice W. Norton; Ginn and Company, "Columbus and the Sailors," "The Echo," "Greedy Ducks," "Spring Music," "The Tree," "Wind Song," all from the *Music Education Series*; Ginn and Company and the editors of *The World of Music*, "The Bell Ringer," "Christmas Is Coming," "Fox and Goose," "Hungarian Dance," "I Am the Wind," "In October," "In Spanish Town," "Indian Dance," "Indian Lullaby," "A Little Bird," "A Magic Fern," "Market Song," "The Mouser," "My Cricket," "My Home's in Montana," "Nine Red Horsemen," "The Pawpaw Patch," "The Polka" (melody only), "Robin Hood and Little John," "Seven Frogs," "The Skaters," "Song before Christmas," "Stories of Travel," "Sung at Harvest Time," "Three Ponies"; Ginn and Company and the editors of *Our Singing World*, "All the Birds Will Soon Be Here," "The Brown Bird," "The Buffalo Head Dance," "Gently the Snow Is Falling," "Haul Away, Joe," "Here Lies a Baby," "Hush, Little Baby," "The Land of the Dutch, Dutch, Dutch," "Night Herding Song," "The Polka" (words only), "Rosa," "Susan Blue," "Up Yonder"; Ginn and Company and the editors of *Faith and Freedom*, "Our Lady of the Seas" (words only) by Dr. Mary Synon; Hall & McCreary Company, text of "Step Softly, Little Donkey" from *Father, Hear Thy Children Sing*, Copyright 1953 by Hall & McCreary Company, used by permission; *Little Mine*, Publications for Catholic Youth, "A Little Squirrel" (words only) by Ethel Hopper; Sheed and Ward, "Our Lady" by Marigold Hunt, from *Gospel Rhymes, An Anthology*, copyright 1934 Sheed and Ward, Inc., New York; Yale University Press, "Windmill" (words only) from John Farrar's *Songs for Parents*.

The melodic setting of "A Little Squirrel" is used by courtesy of Sister Wilhelmina, D.C.

In the case of some poems for which acknowledgment is not given, we have earnestly endeavored to find the original source and to procure permission for their use, but without success.

The contents of this book have received the approval of the DIOCESAN MUSIC COMMISSION, Boston, Massachusetts.

DEDICATION

*This book is dedicated
to St. Pius X,
friend of children the world over.*

Contents

AFTER PENTECOST

Great God of Love, 7
Holy Mary, Blessèd Mary, 8
I Listen to the Whistles, 8
The Rain, 9
Grasshopper Green, 10
Windmill, 11
The Swan Boats, 12
Our School Bus, 13
Music, 14
Two Little Clouds, 15
The Wind, 15
The Polka, 16
Fox and Goose, 17
A Little Squirrel, 18
Autumn Leaves, 18
Indian Summer Days, 19
Columbus and the Sailors, 19
We Sing the Mass, 20
Little Willie, 22
Wind and Rain, 23
In October, 24
America, 24
O Land So Beautiful, 25
Nine Red Horsemen, 26
Dancing Long Ago, 27
To Christ the King, 28
Gloria Patri, 28
Evening Prayer, 28
All Through the Night, 29
Geography Travels, 30
Morning Song, 31
Maiden Mother, Meek and Mild, 32
Holy Mother, 32
Maiden Mother, Meek and Mild (Chant notation), 33
Salve Mater, 33
Jack O'Lantern, 34
The Master Weaver, 35
Christus Vincit, 36
Agnus Dei, 36
Agnus Dei (Chant notation), 36
Taps, 37
The Drummer Boy, 37
My Home's in Montana, 38
Night Herding Song, 39
Go to Sleep, My Baby, 40
Golden Slumbers, 41
Pedro and the Goats, 42
Sung at Harvest Time, 43
Canticle of Praise, 44
Thanksgiving Song, 44
Seek Ye the Lord, 45
Bless the Lord, 45

ADVENT

O Come, O Come, Emmanuel, 46
Soon Will the Christ Child Come, 47
The Advent Wreath, 48
The Jay Birds, 50
If I Had a Nickel, 50
Three Ponies, 51
The Hunters, 52
Brother, Come and Dance, 53
The Snow, 54
Bye, Baby, Bye, 55
Song before Christmas, 56
Christmas Is Coming, 57
Jingle Bells, 58
Stories of Travel, 59
O Salutaris, 60
Protect Us, O Lord, 60
Sanctus—Benedictus, 61

CHRISTMASTIDE AND AFTER

Adeste Fideles, 62
A Christmas Song, 64
Silent Night, 65
A Child Is Born in Bethlehem, 66
Lovely Infant, 66
The Friendly Beasts, 67
Christmas Blessings, 68
Mary's Child Was Jesus, 69
Come to the Manger, 70
Here Lies a Baby, 71
Lullaby to the Infant Jesus, 72
The Three Kings (Play), 74
   A Bright New Star, 74
   The Kings Are Riding over the Mountains, 75
   Suddenly the Star Disappears! 76
Oh! Where Is Our Wonderful Star? 76
Bethlehem, the City of David, 77
Down to Bethlehem Now the Caravan Goes, 78
Kneeling Down They Adore Him, 79
Gold I Bring for a King, 80
Frankincense I Bring to Christ, Our Lord, 80
Myrrh Is the Gift I Bring, 81
Far Away, the Kings Are Far Away, 82
Jesus Born in Bethlehem, 82
Step Softly, Little Donkey, 83
New Year, 84
Reuben and Rachel, 85
The Skaters, 86
Jesu dulcis memoria, 88
O Jesus, Lord, Thy Holy Name, 88
Morning Hymn, 89
Evening Hymn, 89
Gently the Snow Is Falling, 90
Saint Peter, 90
Prayer for a Little Child, 91
On the Road to Damascus, 91
The Schooner Sally, 92
We Built a Snowman in the Yard, 92
Haul Away, Joe, 93
Our Lady's Lullaby, 94
Our Lady's Children, 94

A Valentine Surprise, 95
Our Country, 96
Yankee Doodle, 97
Under the Snow, 98
Falling Snow, 99
Franz Joseph Haydn: Biographical Sketch, 100
Thanks to Our God, 100
Country Dance, 101
A New Created World, 102
The Heavens Are Telling, 102

LENT AND PASSIONTIDE

Stabat Mater, 103
Parce Domine, 103
Kyrie Eleison, 104
Joseph, Our Protector, 104
Saint Joseph's Song, 105
I Am the Wind, 106
There Was a Little Ship, 106
I'm Glad, 107
I'm the Doctor Eisenbart, 108
The Busy Tailors, 109
Seven Frogs, 110
My Cricket, 110
Robin Hood and Little John, 111
The Annunciation, 112
Mother of Christ, 113
Forgive Us Our Sins, O Lord, 113
The River, 114
The Tree, 114
Down in the Valley, 115
Old Folks at Home, 116
Ring, Ring the Banjo! 117
'Liza Jane, 118
The Pawpaw Patch, 119

EASTER

Alleluia, 120
O Filii et Filiae, 120
Hymn of Praise, 121
At Easter Time, 121
Three Little Chickens, 122
Greedy Ducks, 123
The Land of the Dutch, Dutch, Dutch, 124
Spring Music, 125
Four in a Boat, 126
Have You Ever Seen the Daisies? 127
The Mother Moon, 127
All the Birds Will Soon Be Here, 128
The Bumblebee, 128
The Brown Bird, 129
Old Man Thunder, 130
The Rainbow, 131
The Four Winds, 131
Little Brown Brother, 132
Indian Lullaby, 132
Jesus, Tender Shepherd, Hear Me, 133
Home on the Range, 134
While the Balalaikas Play, 135
Up Yonder, 136
Hungarian Dance, 137
Hickory, Dickory Dock, 138
The Bell Ringer, 139

PENTECOST

Veni Creator Spiritus, 140
Tantum Ergo, 140
Come, Spirit Blest, 141
I'm a Truck Driver, 142
Market Song, 143
Mockingbird, 144
Bobolink, 144
A Little Bird, 145
Hiking Song, 146
In Spanish Town, 147
The Buffalo Head Dance, 148
Iroquois Song, 149
Indian Dance, 149
Tekakwitha, 150
O Dandelion, 150
Our Lady of the Seas, 151
The Elf, 152
A Magic Fern, 152
The Mouser, 153
Susan Blue, 154
Hush, Little Baby, 155
There Was a Little French Girl, 156
Little Lonely Shepherd, 156
The Echo, 157
Old Dan Tucker, 158
Bedtime, 159
I Asked My Mother for Fifty Cents, 160
Sing, Sing Together, 161
Rosa, 161
Picnic Day, 162
The Star-Spangled Banner, 162
Father Juniper and the Bells of Capistrano (Play), 164
O Mighty God, Father of All, 164
Far Across the Shining Ocean, 165
O Queen of the Heavens, 166
Soon the Bells Will Be Ringing, 167
Mary, Holy Mother, Pray for Us! 168
Holy Mary, Mother of God, 169
Down the Hill Comes a Train of Mules, 170
When the Bells of Capistrano Ring at Golden Dawn of Day, 171
We Sing the Mass, 172

ALPHABETICAL INDEX, 177

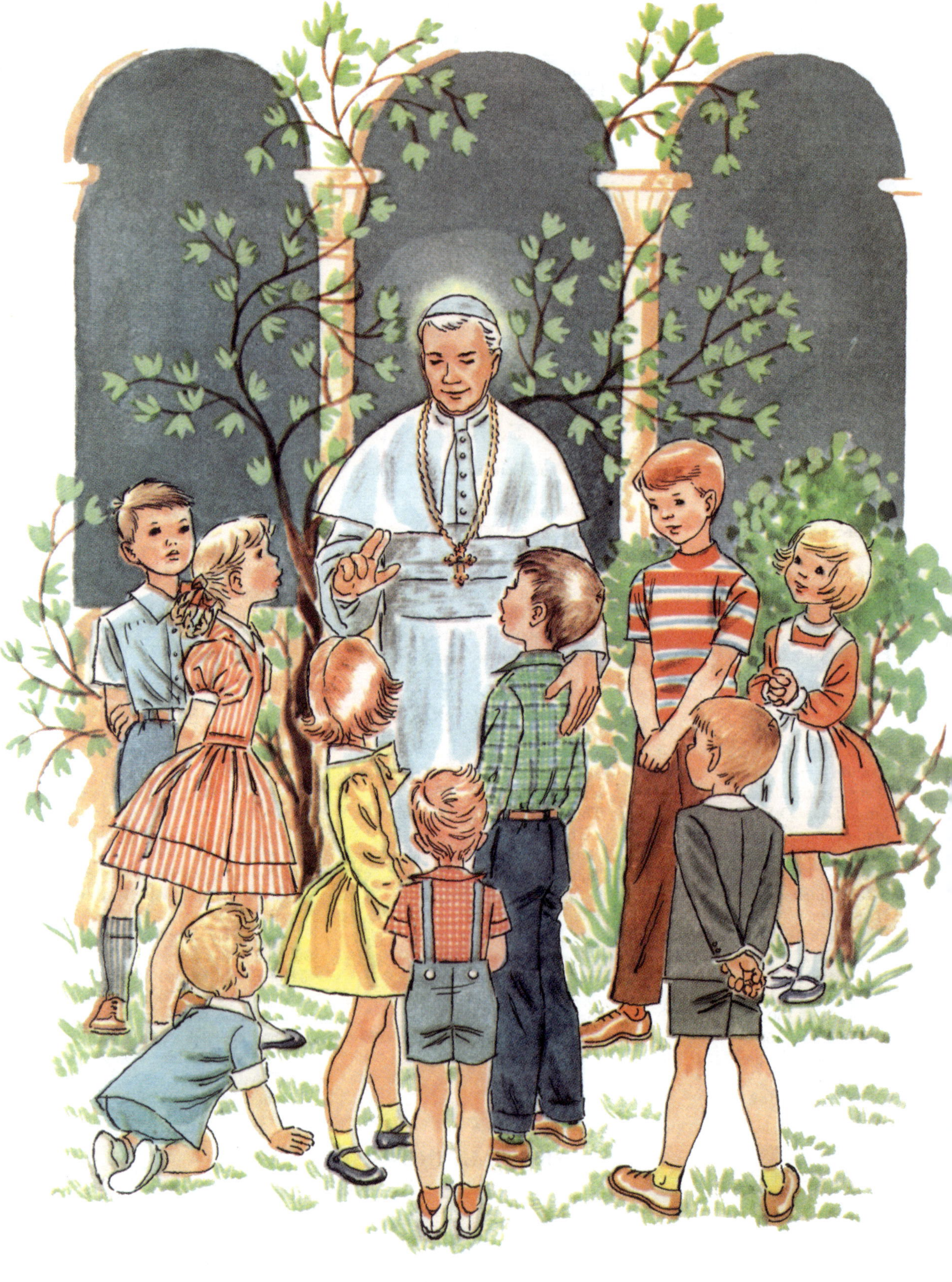

After Pentecost

I will praise Thee, O Lord, with my whole heart,
I will tell of all Thy wondrous works.
Psalm 9

Great God of Love

SISTER JOHN JOSEPH, C.S.J.

Father in Heaven, great God of love,
Hear Thou our plea from Thy home above.
Bless all our dear ones, guide and direct them,
Keep them all faithful, great God of love.

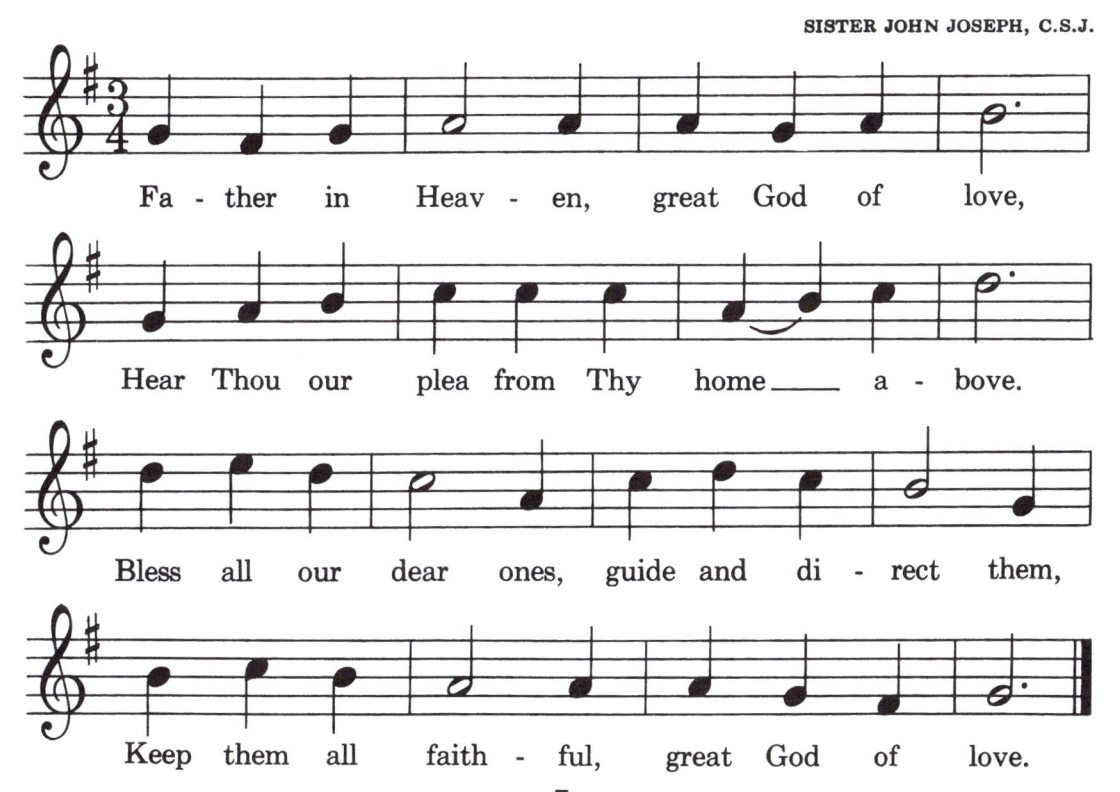

Holy Mary, Blessèd Mary

SISTER JOHN JOSEPH, C.S.J.

Ho-ly Ma-ry, Bless-èd Ma-ry, Moth-er of our Sav-ior,

Ho-ly Ma-ry, Bless-èd Ma-ry lis-ten to our pray'r.

Pur-est lil-y, spot-less Vir-gin, Queen of all the an-gels,

Ho-ly Vir-gin, Ho-ly Moth-er lis-ten to our plead-ing,

Lis-ten to our pray'r.

I Listen to the Whistles

SISTER ROSE MARGARET, C.S.J.

1. I lis-ten to the whis-tles from my win-dow on the street,
2. I hear the lit-tle tug-boats and the o-cean lin-ers too,

Oo ___
Whoo ___

I lis-ten to the whis-tles when it's hard to go to sleep,
The lit-tle tugs say, "Toot-toot," and the o-cean lin-ers, "Whoo."

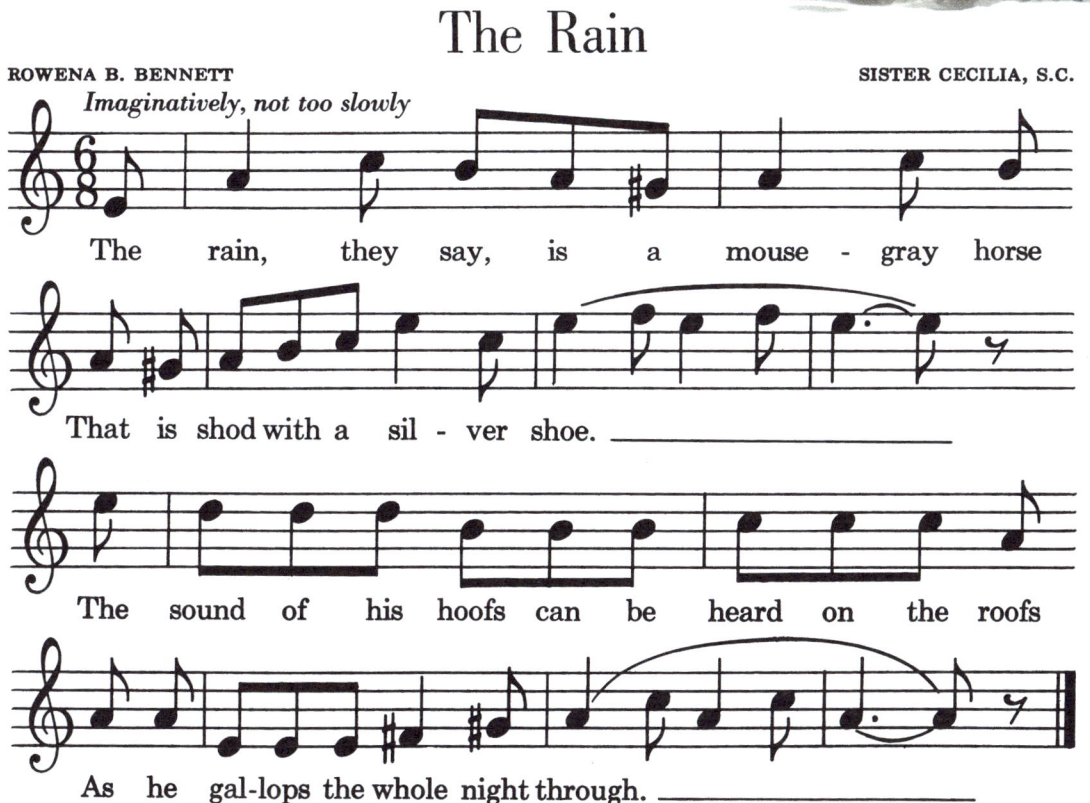

Oo ___
Whoo ___

The Rain

ROWENA B. BENNETT　　　　　　　　　　　　　　　SISTER CECILIA, S.C.

Imaginatively, not too slowly

The rain, they say, is a mouse-gray horse

That is shod with a sil-ver shoe. ___

The sound of his hoofs can be heard on the roofs

As he gal-lops the whole night through. ___

Grasshopper Green

UNKNOWN
GERMAN FOLK TUNE

1. Grass - hop - per green is a com - ic - al chap:
2. Grass - hop - per green has a quaint lit - tle house;

He lives on the best of fare.
It's un - der the hedge so gay,

Bright lit - tle trou - sers, jack - et and cap,
Grand - moth - er Spi - der, still as a mouse,

These are his sum - mer wear.
Watch - es him o'er the way.

Out in the mead - ow he loves to go,
Glad - ly he's call - ing us all, I know,

Play - ing a - way in the sun;
Out in the beau - ti - ful sun;

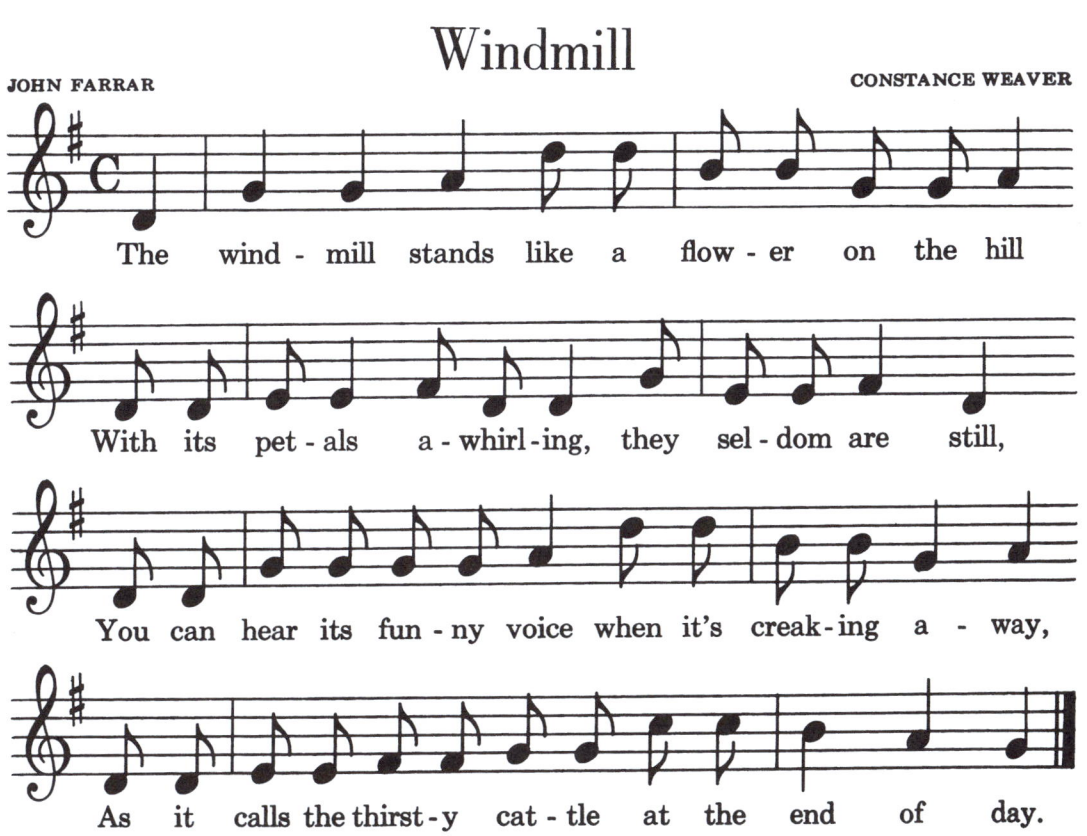

It's hop-per-ty skip-per-ty, high and low.
It's hop-per-ty skip-per-ty, high and low.

Sum-mer's the time for fun.
Sum-mer's the time for fun.

Windmill

JOHN FARRAR CONSTANCE WEAVER

The wind-mill stands like a flow-er on the hill

With its pet-als a-whirl-ing, they sel-dom are still,

You can hear its fun-ny voice when it's creak-ing a-way,

As it calls the thirst-y cat-tle at the end of day.

Which two phrases are almost alike?

The Swan Boats

FRENCH FOLK TUNE

O-ver the lake the swan boats are sail-ing,

Smooth-ly and slow up-on the wa-ter clear.

Safe in the boat hap-py chil-dren are rid-ing,

Feed-ing the ducks on the smooth wa-ter glid-ing.

Swan boats are slow, state-ly and slow.

Find the phrases that are alike.

Our School Bus

SCALE SONG

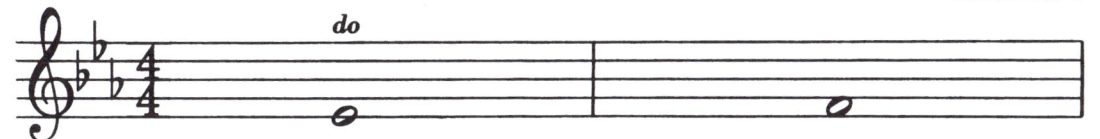

do
John gets on at the corner stop. Sue gets on at the candy shop.

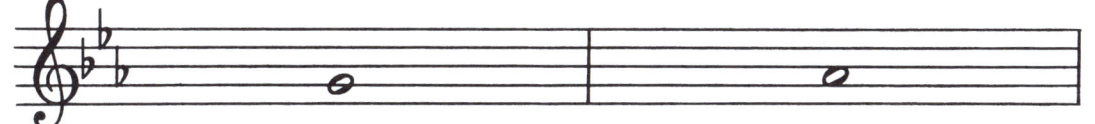

Bill comes running, we have to wait. Ann is never - well, hardly ever - late.

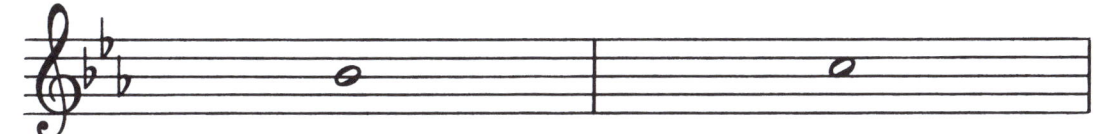

Joe lives right at the top of the hill. Hurry up, Jack, we can't stand still.

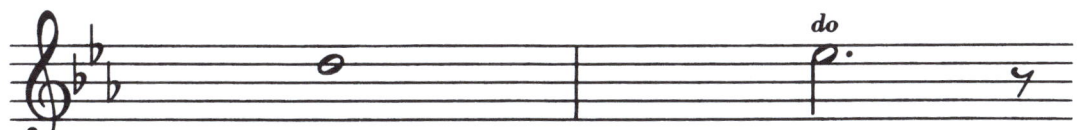

do
Jane has two little brothers to bring. Everybody on! We laugh and sing!

do ti la so fa mi re do
"Toot - toot," we're on our way to school!

Sing all the music syllables before you sing the words.

Music

Paraphrased by S. C.
CZECH FOLK SONG

1. Mu - sic for play - ing, tra la la la lee!
2. Mu - sic for danc - ing, tra la la la lee!

Mu - sic for sing - ing, tra la la la lee!
Gay mu - sic danc - ing, tra la la la lee!

How we love to hear the fid - dle play this hap - py mel - o - dy.
How we love to step the rhy - thm of this hap - py mel - o - dy.

Most of all we love to sing tra la la la la lee.
Whirl - ing, twirl - ing as we sing tra la la la la lee.

The first and second phrases sound somewhat alike, but the second phrase is higher.

How do the third and fourth phrases differ?

14

Two Little Clouds

KATIE VANDER ZANDEN

Two lit-tle clouds one sum-mer day Went fly-ing through the sky,—
They went so fast they bumped their heads And both be-gan to cry.—
Old Fa-ther Sun looked out and said, "Oh, nev-er mind, my dears,—
I'll send my lit-tle sun-beams down To dry your fall-ing tears."—

The Wind

S. C.
SPANISH FOLK TUNE

mi ti re do la so mi re mi fa re ti so do

1. Wind blow-ing from the moun-tain In the qui-et of the night,—
2. Wind blow-ing from the o-cean When the morn-ing's break-ing gray,—

Oh, sing, sing me of the moun-tain And the snow-y peaks so white.
Oh, sing, sing me of the o-cean And the salt-y o-cean spray.

After you know this song, sing all of it with music syllables.

15

The Polka

CHRISTINE TURNER CURTIS   RUSSIAN FOLK TUNE

1. Step, step, step, hop, step, step, step, hop, This is called the pol-ka dance.
2. Mer-ry pol-kas, mer-ry pol-kas Rus-sian peo-ple love to dance.
3. From the farm-yard, from the farm-yard Pol-kas sound on sum-mer nights.

Step, step, step, hop with a part-ner, All move clock-wise, smile and glance.
Three steps for-ward, three steps for-ward, Then a kind of hop and prance.
In the mead-ows, in the mead-ows Fire-flies hang their yel-low lights.

Stamp, stamp, heel and toe, Then go on with pol-ka slow;
Bal - a - lai-kas cry, Cheeks grow red and sash-es fly.
Three steps, then a hop, On they dance and can-not stop.

Stamp, stamp, heel and toe, And re-peat the dance just so.
Girls wear crim-son boots, Boys wear blous-es with their suits.
Day breaks on the hill, Yet the crowds are danc-ing still.

Look at the time signature. The upper number tells you there are two beats in a measure. Tap twice to each measure while you sing.

The words of the first stanza tell you how to do this dance.

Fox and Goose

Translated by CECIL COWDREY
GERMAN FOLK SONG

1. Fox, you stole my neigh-bor's goose, sir, Bet-ter bring it back, Bet-ter bring it back.
2. Lit-tle fox, look out for dan-ger, Steal-ing will not do, Steal-ing will not do.

There's a hunt-er watch-ing you, sir, Wait-ing close up-on your track;
You had bet-ter be a stran-ger To the goose who's not for you;

There's a hunt-er watch-ing you, sir, Close up-on your track.
You had bet-ter be a stran-ger, Goose is not for you.

A sharp looks like this. (♯) Notice that there are four sharps at the beginning of each staff. They tell you that *do* is on the first line of the staff.

A Little Squirrel

ETHEL HOPPER
SISTER WILHELMINA, D.C.

Lively

1. A lit-tle squirr'l runs up and down in our big wal-nut tree.
2. My moth-er says he stores them safe for food when north winds blow.

All day he car-ries nuts a-way, as bus-y as can be.
I won-der how the squirr'l knows that some day we'll have snow.

Tap once for each quarter note and twice for each half note.
Remember to tap once for each quarter rest.

Autumn Leaves

do   *do*   *ti*

Au-tumn leaves are blow-ing, down the street they're blow-ing;

fa mi re so fa mi

Red and gold, dust-y brown, from the trees tum-bling down.

fa

When the wind comes whis-tling by, all the leaves go sail-ing high.

A flat looks like this. (♭) When there is one flat at the beginning of a song, *do* is always in the first space.

Sing the whole song with syllables before you sing the words.

18

Indian Summer Days

MARYBETH BAYLEY
LUDWIG VAN BEETHOVEN

1. Gold - en and brown, now the leaves are drift - ing down,
2. Moun - tains are veiled in the pur - ple au - tumn haze.

Blue is the sky, snow - y clouds are sail - ing high.
Dream - y and warm are the In - dian sum - mer days.

Sing all of this song with music syllables before you sing the words.

Columbus and the Sailors

MARY STANHOPE
FOLK TUNE

1. The sail - ors of Co - lum - bus said, "We're wea - ry of the main,
2. So brave Co - lum - bus said, "My lads, be pa - tient, one day more!

Of o - cean in com - mo - tion; o - cean, mo - tion!
Why do you bor - row sor - row, bor - row sor - row?

O sir, it is our no - tion to sail right back to Spain."
Just wait un - til to - mor - row and we shall see the shore."

Sing all of this song with music syllables. Remember there is only one beat for two eighth notes. (♪) How many times will you tap in a measure?

We Sing the Mass

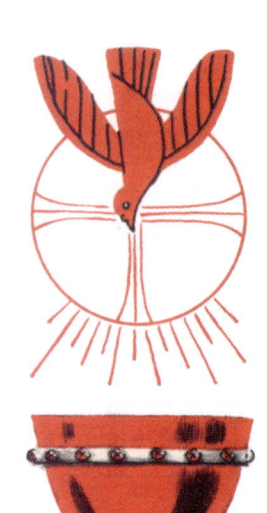

When we sing the Mass we receive a greater share in its blessings. Boys and girls in the fourth grade are old enough to participate in singing part of the Mass. A good place to begin is with the *Preface*, which is the introduction to the most important part of the Mass, called the *Canon of the Mass*.

The Preface is like a conversation between the priest and the people. The priest first asks the people to join him in singing the praises of God. Then he sings a beautiful hymn of praise and thanksgiving to the Most Blessèd Trinity. At the end of the hymn the people (or the choir) sing, *"Holy, Holy, Holy, Lord God of Hosts! Heaven and Earth Are Full of Thy Glory!"*

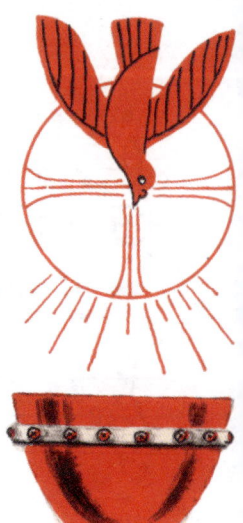

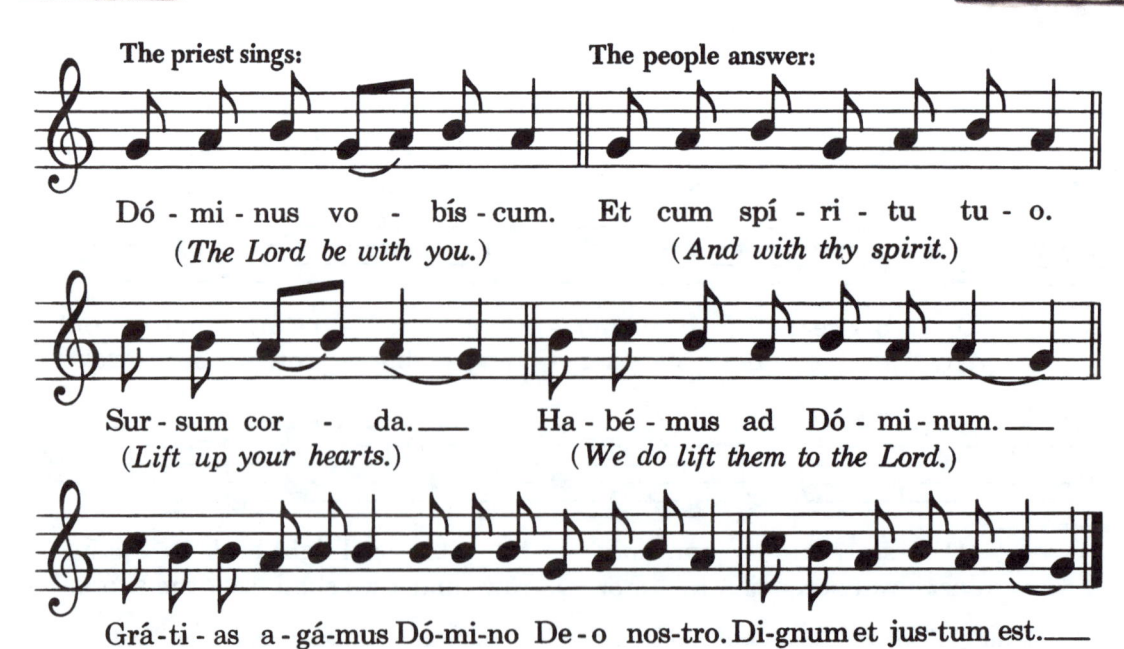

The priest sings: Dó - mi - nus vo - bís - cum.
(The Lord be with you.)

The people answer: Et cum spí - ri - tu tu - o.
(And with thy spirit.)

Sur - sum cor - da.
(Lift up your hearts.)

Ha - bé - mus ad Dó - mi - num.
(We do lift them to the Lord.)

Grá - ti - as a - gá - mus Dó - mi - no De - o nos - tro.
(Let us give thanks to the Lord, our God.)

Di - gnum et jus - tum est.
(It is fitting and just.)

Priest: It is truly fitting and just, right and availing unto salvation, that we should at all times, and in all places, give thanks unto Thee, O Holy Lord, Father Almighty, and Everlasting God, through Christ, Our Lord. Through Whom the angels praise Thy majesty, the dominions worship it, the powers stand in awe. The heavens, and the heavenly hosts, and the blessed seraphim join together in celebrating their joy. We pray Thee to join our voices with theirs as we sing with humble praise:

Sanctus

MASS XVIII

Sán-ctus,＿ Sán-ctus,＿ Sán-ctus Dó-mi-nus Dé-us Sá-ba-oth.
(*Holy, Holy, Holy, Lord God of Hosts.*)

Plé-ni sunt caé-li et tér-ra gló-ri-a tú-a.
(*Heaven and earth are filled with Thy glory.*)

Ho-sán-na in ex-cél-sis. Be-ne-díc-tus qui vé-nit
(*Hosanna in the highest.*) (*Blessèd is He Who comes

in nó-mi-ne Dó-mi-ni. Ho-san-na in ex-cél-sis.＿
in the name of the Lord.*) (*Hosanna in the highest.*)

Little Willie

OLD AMERICAN

1. Lit-tle Wil-lie stood un-der the ap-ple tree old,
2. He stretched out his hand to the rip-est one there,

The fruit was all shin-y and crim-son and gold,
But just then a voice seemed to say from some-where,

So tempt-ing-ly low, and he longed for a bite,
"Oh, Wil-lie, don't touch the ap-ple so red,

But he knew if he took one it would not be right.
Re-mem-ber to do as your dear fa-ther said."

He said, "I don't see why my fa-ther should say,
Then Wil-lie turned round just as still as a mouse,

Don't touch the old ap-ple tree, Wil-lie, to-day."
Crept soft-ly and si-lent-ly in-to the house.

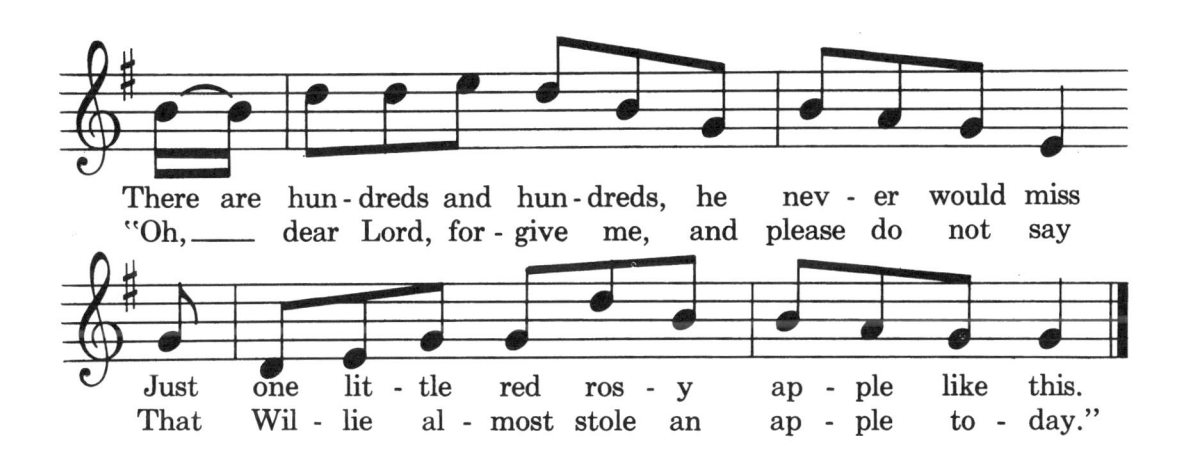

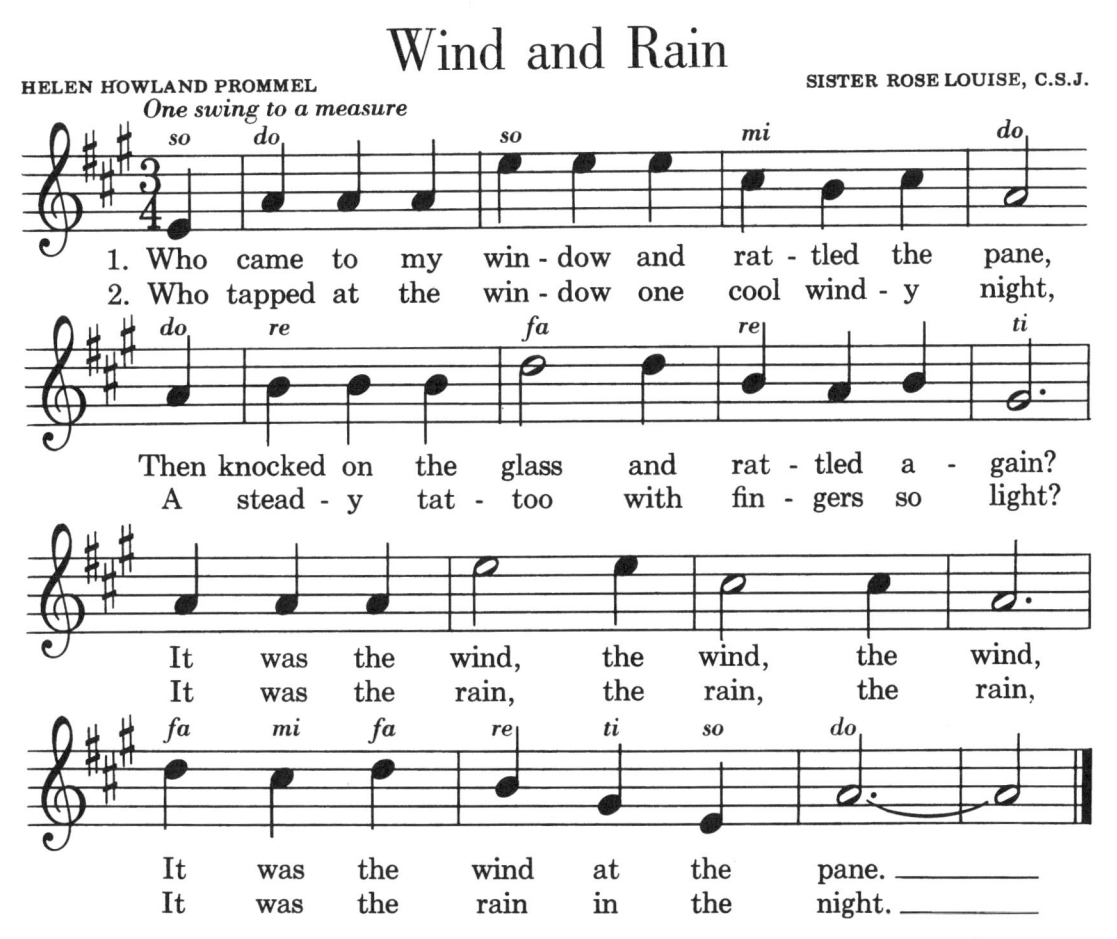

There are hun - dreds and hun - dreds, he nev - er would miss
"Oh,___ dear Lord, for - give me, and please do not say

Just one lit - tle red ros - y ap - ple like this.
That Wil - lie al - most stole an ap - ple to - day."

Wind and Rain

HELEN HOWLAND PROMMEL
SISTER ROSE LOUISE, C.S.J.

One swing to a measure

1. Who came to my win - dow and rat - tled the pane,
2. Who tapped at the win - dow one cool wind - y night,

Then knocked on the glass and rat - tled a - gain?
A stead - y tat - too with fin - gers so light?

It was the wind, the wind, the wind,
It was the rain, the rain, the rain,

It was the wind at the pane. ____
It was the rain in the night. ____

Notice that there are three sharps at the beginning of this song. They tell you that *do* is now in the second space.

Close your eyes and sing the last line with syllables from memory.

In October

LOUISE KESSLER YUGOSLAVIAN FOLK TUNE

1. Man-y days are bright in Oc-to-ber;
2. When the frost is white on the mead-ows,

There is hap-pi-ness in the air.
When the winds of No-vem-ber blow,

Red and yel-low leaves from the au-tumn trees
Then the wild geese fly t'ward the south-ern sky;

Are fall-ing ev-'ry-where.
For soon we shall have snow.

The first note in this song is *so*. Where is *do*?
When there is one sharp at the beginning of a song *do* is on the second line.

America

SAMUEL FRANCIS SMITH TRADITIONAL

1. My coun-try, 'tis of thee, Sweet land of lib-er-ty, Of thee I sing.
2. Our fath-ers' God! to Thee, Au-thor of lib-er-ty, To Thee we sing.

Land where my fa - thers died! Land of the Pil - grims' pride!
Long may our land be bright With free - dom's ho - ly light;
From ev - 'ry moun - tain-side, Let free - dom ring!
Pro - tect us by Thy might, Great God our King!

While you are singing this song clap the rhythm pattern all the way through. Notice how you clap as you sing: ♩ ♩ ♩ | ♩. ♪ ♩ . How many times do you find this rhythm pattern in the song?
"My coun-try, 'tis of thee."

O Land So Beautiful

ST. IRENAEUS SCHOOL
OAKMONT, PENNSYLVANIA

1. O land, so beau - ti - ful, won - der - ful land,
2. We love our beau - ti - ful, won - der - ful land,

With riv - ers and des - erts and seas,
Where peo - ple are hap - py and free!

With moun - tains and hills and cit - ies and towns,
May God bless our land, and keep it from harm,

And prai - ries and for - ests of trees.
And guard our lib - er - ty!

Nine Red Horsemen

ELEANOR FARJEON   MEXICAN FOLK TUNE

1. I ___ saw nine red horse-men Rid-ing o-ver the plain,
2. Their hair streamed be-hind them, And their eyes were a-shine;
3. Their spurs clinked and jin-gled, And their laugh-ter was gay,

And ___ each held his charg-er By its long flow-ing mane.
They ___ all rode as one man, Though I knew there were nine.
And ___ in the red sun-set They all gal-loped a-way.

CHORUS

Tra la la la la la la la! Tra la la la la la la la!
Tra la la la la la la la! Tra la la la la la la la!

What does the time signature tell you?
Tap once for two eighth notes. (♫)
Close your eyes and sing the chorus with music syllables.

Dancing Long Ago

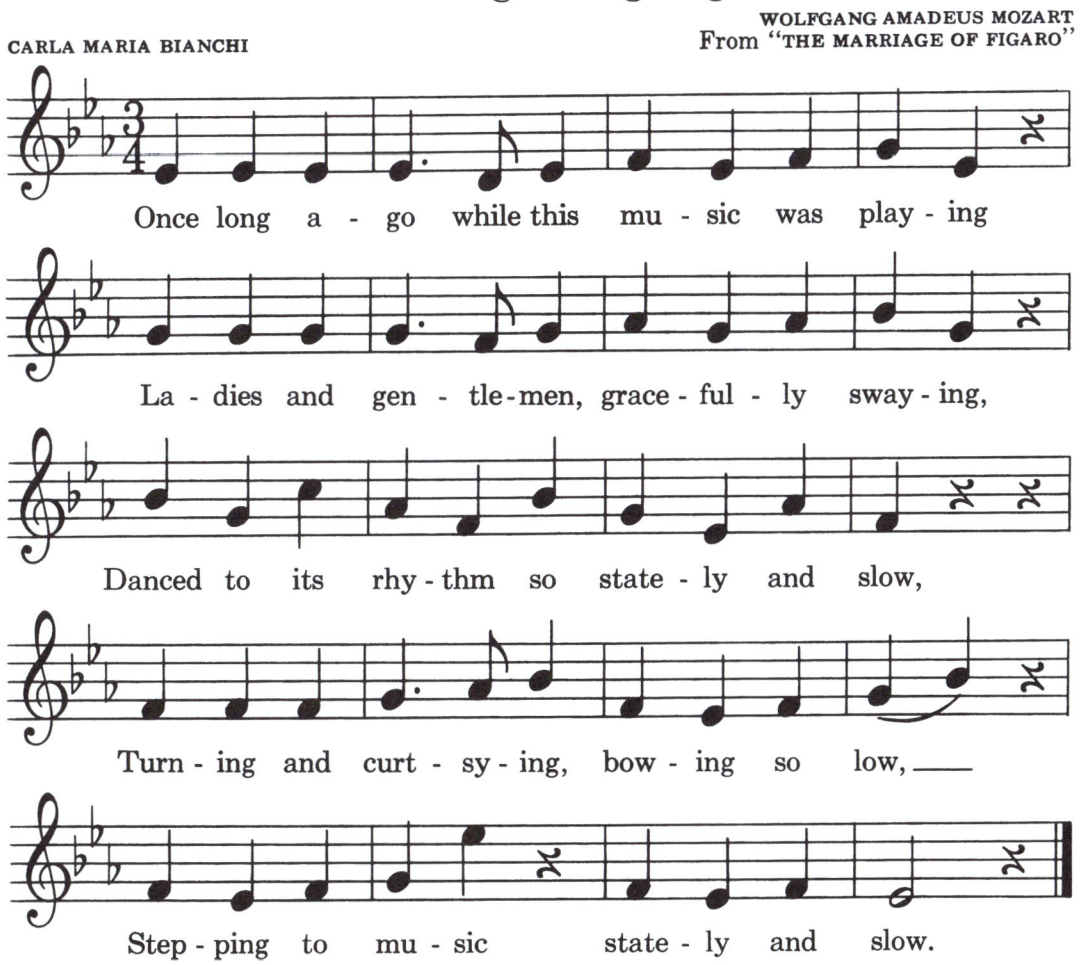

CARLA MARIA BIANCHI

WOLFGANG AMADEUS MOZART
From "THE MARRIAGE OF FIGARO"

Once long a-go while this mu-sic was play-ing

La-dies and gen-tle-men, grace-ful-ly sway-ing,

Danced to its rhy-thm so state-ly and slow,

Turn-ing and curt-sy-ing, bow-ing so low,——

Step-ping to mu-sic state-ly and slow.

How many times do you find this rhythm pattern? (♩. ♪ ♩)
Notice that the rhythm pattern for "liberty" in "America" is the same.
Clap this pattern or play it on a wood block or with rhythm sticks.

Thou, O Christ, art the King of Glory.

To Christ the King

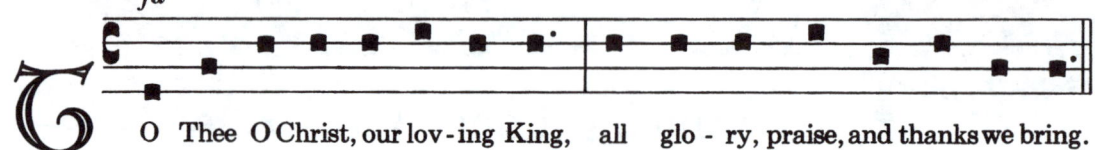

fa

O Thee O Christ, our lov-ing King, all glo-ry, praise, and thanks we bring.
All glo-ry as is ev-er meet, to Fa-ther and to Pa-ra-clete.

This is the way Gregorian Chant is written. Do you notice that the staff has only four lines and that the notes are square?
Below you will see the same chant with Latin words.

Gloria Patri

fa

Ló-ri-a Pá-tri et Fí-li-o et Spi-rí-tu-i Sán-cto.
(Glory be to the Father and to the Son and to the Holy Spirit.)

Evening Prayer

JAN BEZDEK   NORWEGIAN FOLK TUNE

With reverence

1. God our Fa-ther, God our Light, God of maj-es-ty and might!
2. Love e-ter-nal, love di-vine, Lead our hearts to love but Thine.

Take our souls and bod-ies too, All we have, we owe to You.
Glo-ry, hon-or, ser-vice too, These we will to give to You.

Bless us, keep us through this night, God our Fa-ther, God our Light.
Bless our fam-'lies, make them Thine. Love e-ter-nal, love di-vine.

Four sharps tell you that *do* is on the first line.
Do you know how to tap this rhythm pattern? (♩. ♪ ♩ ♩)
How does it differ from "liberty" in "America," p. 24?

All Through the Night

SIR HAROLD BOULTON   WELSH FOLK SONG

1. Sleep, my child, and peace at-tend thee   All through the night!
2. While the moon her watch is keep-ing   All through the night!

Guard-ian an-gels God will send thee   All through the night!
While the wea-ry world is sleep-ing   All through the night!

Soft the drow-sy hours are creep-ing, Hill and vale in slum-ber steep-ing;
O'er thy spir-it gen-tly steal-ing, Vi-sions of de-light re-veal-ing,

I my lov-ing vig-il keep-ing   All through the night!
Breathes a pure and ho-ly feel-ing   All through the night!

How many times can you find ♩. ♪ ♩ ♩ in this song?

29

Geography Travels

SHEILA GALVIN   FOLK TUNE

1. We trav - el fast, we trav - el far,
2. We see the mag - ic mid - night sun,
3. To peo - ple near or far a - way

We trav - el past the far - thest star,
We watch the Con - go riv - er run,
We have a pleas - ant word to say,

A - cross the land, a - cross the sea
We ride a - cross the des - ert sands
For they are all the friends, you see,

We go in our ge - og - ra - phy.
To vis - it strange and dis - tant lands.
We've met in our ge - og - ra - phy.

In how many measures do you find a dotted quarter note followed by an eighth? (♩. ♪) Do you know how to sing this rhythm pattern?

Morning Song

SISTER CECILIA, S.C.   SPANISH FOLK TUNE
One swing to each measure

Now the sun in the morn - ing sky

Shines so bright on the moun - tain high.

Hear the bells in the stee - ple with sil - ver - y sound,

See the doves from the stee - ple go wheel-ing a - round,

All the shad-ows have flown a - way,

Praise the Lord for this gold - en day.

Do you notice that there are only two tunes in this whole song?

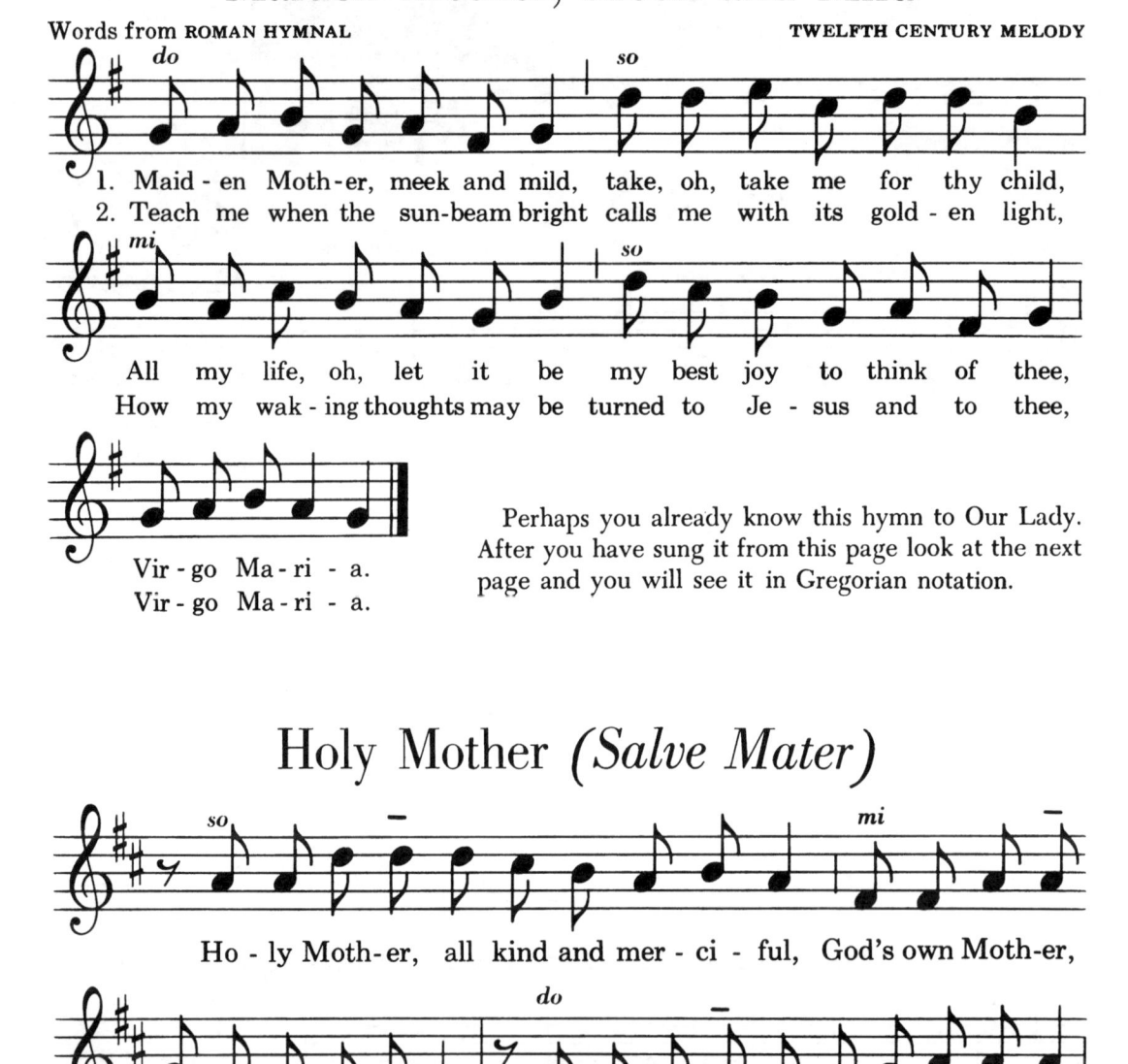

Maiden Mother, Meek and Mild

Words from ROMAN HYMNAL
TWELFTH CENTURY MELODY

1. Maid - en Moth-er, meek and mild, take, oh, take me for thy child,
2. Teach me when the sun-beam bright calls me with its gold - en light,

All my life, oh, let it be my best joy to think of thee,
How my wak - ing thoughts may be turned to Je - sus and to thee,

Vir - go Ma - ri - a.
Vir - go Ma - ri - a.

Perhaps you already know this hymn to Our Lady. After you have sung it from this page look at the next page and you will see it in Gregorian notation.

Holy Mother *(Salve Mater)*

Ho - ly Moth-er, all kind and mer - ci - ful, God's own Moth-er,

O Moth-er boun-ti-ful, Moth-er of hope, O Moth-er full of grace,

Joy - ous Moth-er, our glad-ness plen - ti - ful, O Ma - ri - a.

A short line over a note (♩) tells you to hold the note a little longer. In this hymn be careful to sing these notes lightly.

Maiden Mother, Meek and Mild

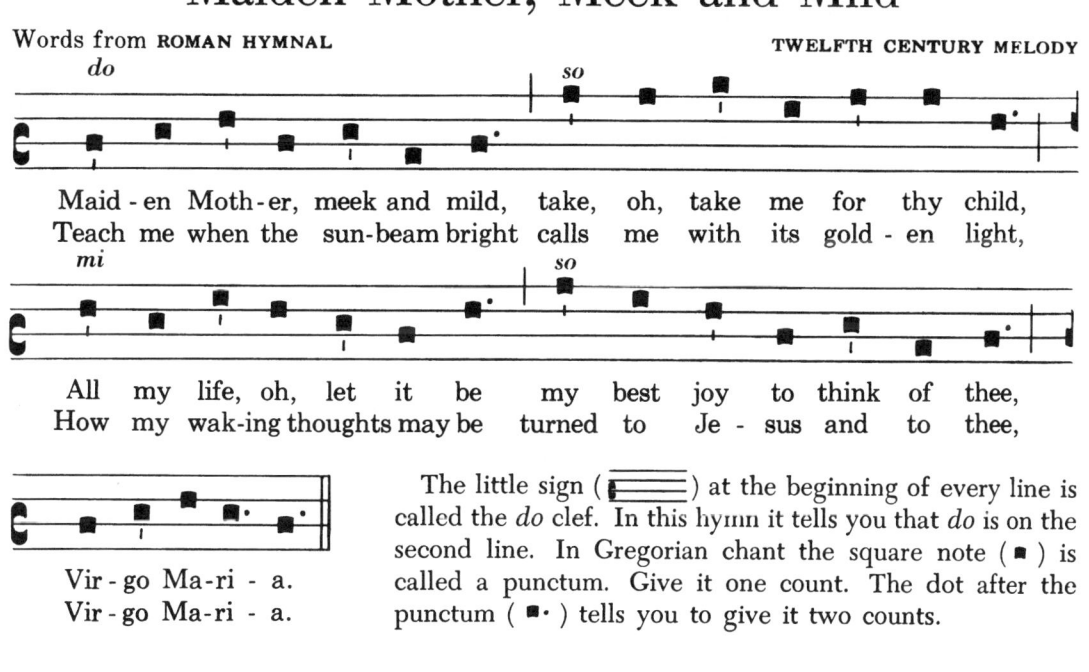

Words from ROMAN HYMNAL
TWELFTH CENTURY MELODY

Maid-en Moth-er, meek and mild, take, oh, take me for thy child,
Teach me when the sun-beam bright calls me with its gold-en light,

All my life, oh, let it be my best joy to think of thee,
How my wak-ing thoughts may be turned to Je-sus and to thee,

Vir-go Ma-ri-a.
Vir-go Ma-ri-a.

The little sign ( ) at the beginning of every line is called the *do* clef. In this hymn it tells you that *do* is on the second line. In Gregorian chant the square note (■) is called a punctum. Give it one count. The dot after the punctum (■·) tells you to give it two counts.

Salve Mater

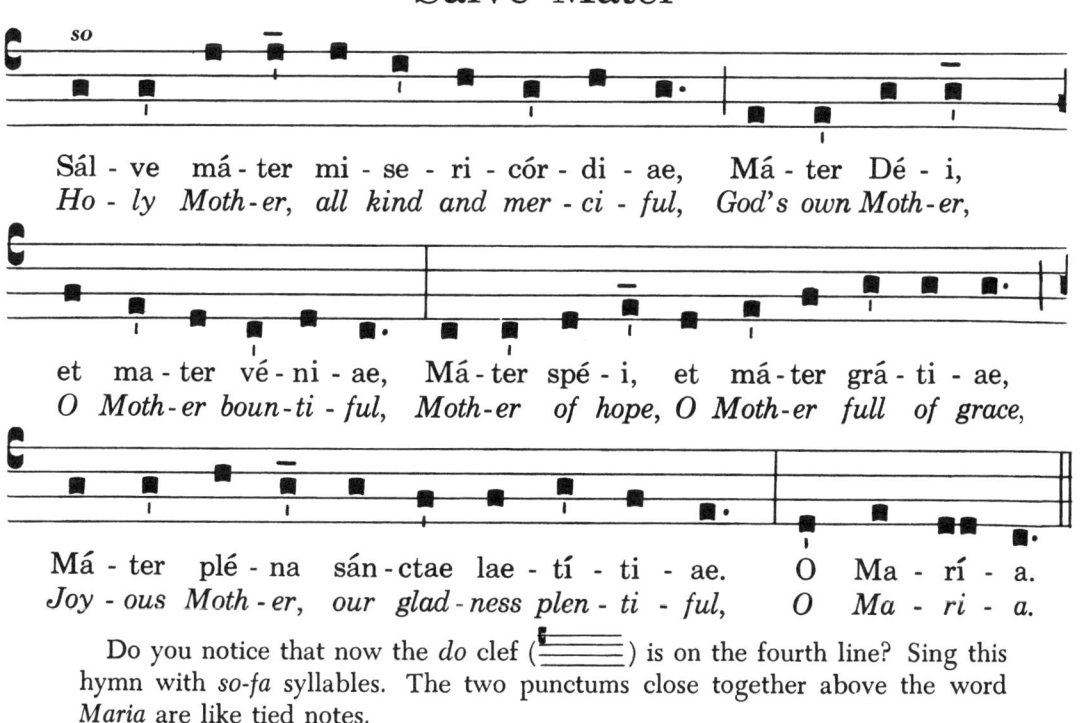

Sál-ve má-ter mi-se-ri-cór-di-ae, Má-ter Dé-i,
Ho-ly Moth-er, all kind and mer-ci-ful, God's own Moth-er,

et ma-ter vé-ni-ae, Má-ter spé-i, et má-ter grá-ti-ae,
O Moth-er boun-ti-ful, Moth-er of hope, O Moth-er full of grace,

Má-ter plé-na sán-ctae lae-tí-ti-ae. O Ma-rí-a.
Joy-ous Moth-er, our glad-ness plen-ti-ful, O Ma-ri-a.

Do you notice that now the *do* clef ( ) is on the fourth line? Sing this hymn with *so-fa* syllables. The two punctums close together above the word *Maria* are like tied notes.

33

Jack O'Lantern

ANNA CHANDLER AYER CONSTANCE WEAVER

The Man in the Moon looked down on the field
Where the gold-en pump-kin lay;
He winked at him and he blinked at him,
But the pump-kin had noth-ing to say.
Yet on Hal-low-een night, when the Moon looked down,
He was rath-er sur-prised at the sight,

For the pump-kin fat on a gate-post sat

And winked with a Hal-low-een light.

The Master Weaver

Translated by DANUTE KANTAUTAS
LITHUANIAN FOLK SONG

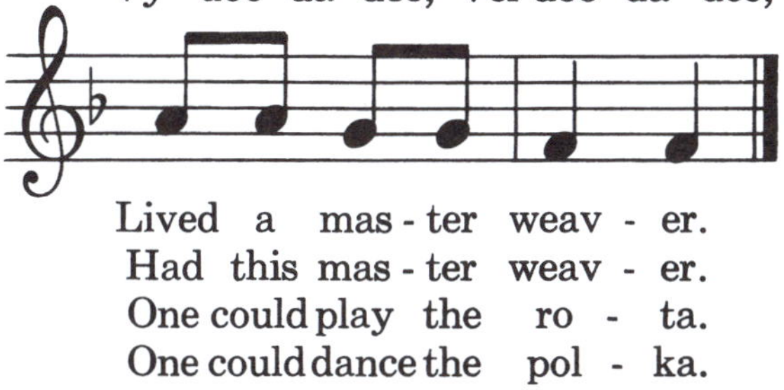

1. In a cot-tage by the road-side lived a mas-ter weav-er,
2. Three fine sons and three fine daugh-ters had this mas-ter weav-er,
3. One could plough and one could sow and one could play the ro-ta,
4. One could cook and one could bake and one could dance the pol-ka,

Vy-doo-da-dee, Vel-doo-da-dee, Vy-doo-da-dee, Vel-doo-da-dee,
Vy-doo-da-dee, Vel-doo-da-dee, Vy-doo-da-dee, Vel-doo-da-dee,
Vy-doo-da-dee, Vel-doo-da-dee, Vy-doo-da-dee, Vel-doo-da-dee,
Vy-doo-da-dee, Vel-doo-da-dee, Vy-doo-da-dee, Vel-doo-da-dee,

Lived a mas-ter weav-er.
Had this mas-ter weav-er.
One could play the ro-ta.
One could dance the pol-ka.

What does the time signature in this song tell you?
The rota is an old musical instrument.

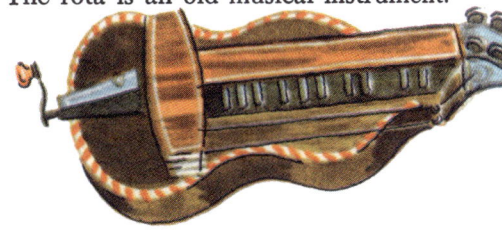

Christus Vincit

la

Chri-stus vin-cit, Chri-stus re-gnat, Chri-stus ím-pe-rat.
(*Christ conquers, Christ reigns, Christ commands.*)

A group of two or more notes sung on the same vowel is called a *neum*. This two-note group is a neum. It is called a *clivis*.

Agnus Dei

MASS XVIII

so

1-2. A-gnus Dé - i,* qui tól-lis pec-cá-ta mún-di: mi-se-ré-re nó-bis. *ij.*

3. A-gnus Dé - i,* qui tól-lis pec-cá-ta mún-di: dó-na nó-bis pá-cem.

Perhaps you remember singing and seeing the "Agnus Dei" above when you were in third grade. The same chant appears below in Gregorian notation. Notice the neum over "Dei" ( ). It is called a *podatus* and the lower note is sung first.

Agnus Dei

MASS XVIII

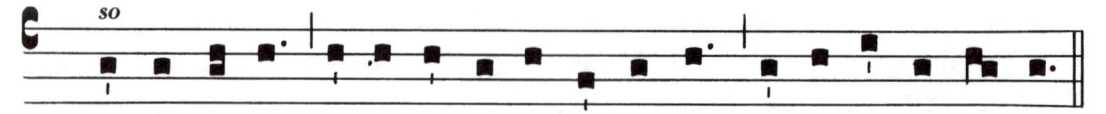

so

1-2. A-gnus Dé - i,* qui tól-lis pec-cá-ta mún-di: mi-se-ré-re nó-bis. *ij.*

3. A-gnus Dé - i,* qui tól-lis pec-cá-ta mún-di: dó-na nó-bis pá-cem.

Taps

U. S. ARMY BUGLE CALL

so do mi

Day is done, gone the sun from the lake, from the hill, from the sky,

All is well, safe-ly rest, God is nigh.

Do you notice that all the notes in this bugle call are *do, mi* and *so*?

The Drummer Boy

SUSAN RIES GERMAN FOLK TUNE

I like to play my big bass drum, play my big bass drum;

The peo-ple cheer me as I come, boom-da-da, boom-da-da, boom, boom, boom.

Oh, hear the beat-ing, hear the beat-ing of the drum!

I like to play the drum, boom-da, boom-da, boom-da, boom.

My Home's in Montana

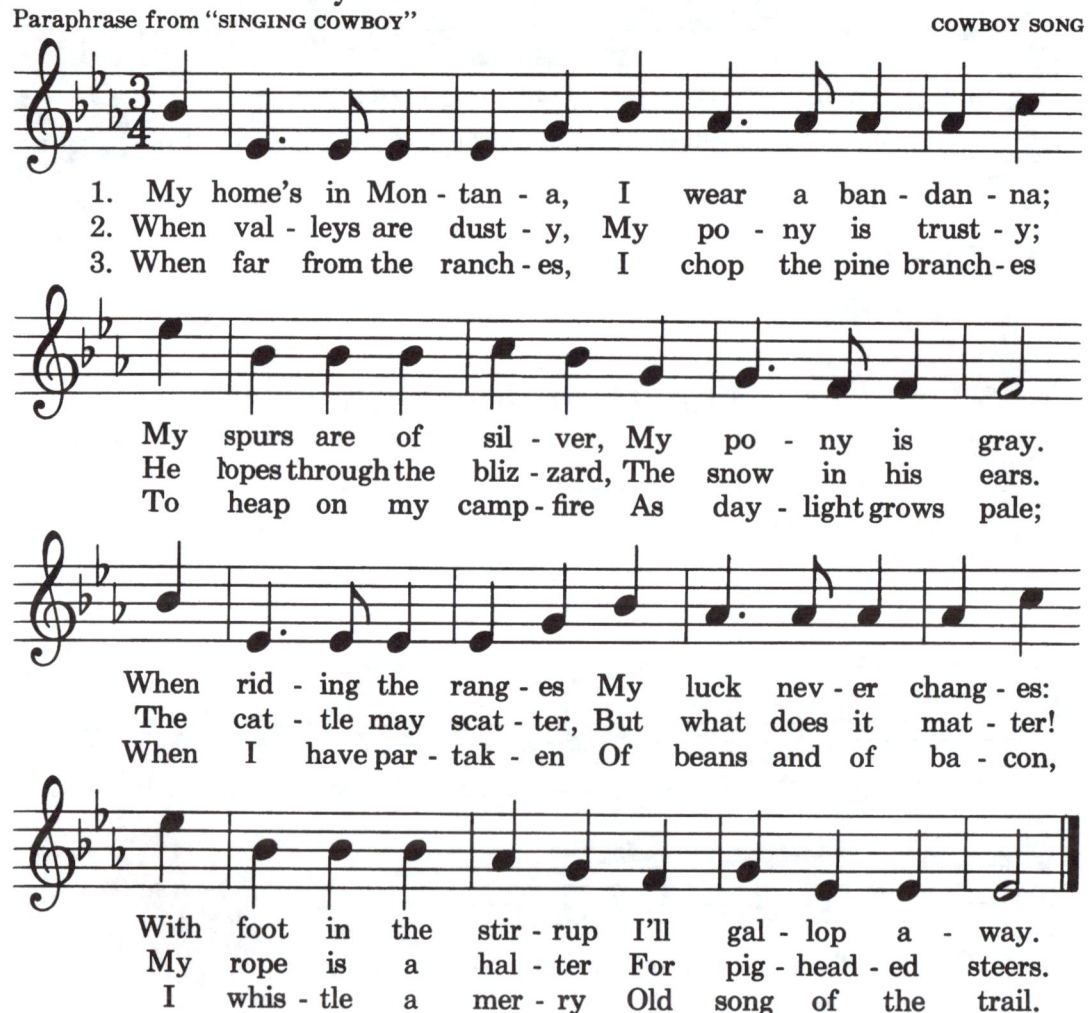

Paraphrase from "SINGING COWBOY"
COWBOY SONG

1. My home's in Mon-tan-a, I wear a ban-dan-na;
2. When val-leys are dust-y, My po-ny is trust-y;
3. When far from the ranch-es, I chop the pine branch-es

My spurs are of sil-ver, My po-ny is gray.
He lopes through the bliz-zard, The snow in his ears.
To heap on my camp-fire As day-light grows pale;

When rid-ing the rang-es My luck nev-er chang-es:
The cat-tle may scat-ter, But what does it mat-ter!
When I have par-tak-en Of beans and of ba-con,

With foot in the stir-rup I'll gal-lop a-way.
My rope is a hal-ter For pig-head-ed steers.
I whis-tle a mer-ry Old song of the trail.

Be sure to sing correctly the dotted quarter note followed by an eighth note every time you see it in this song.

When there are three flats *do* is on the first line. Do you remember that *do* is also on the first line when there are four sharps?

Night Herding Song

COWBOY SONG

1. Oh say, little dogies, quit roving around,
   You've wandered and trampled all over the ground.
   Oh, graze along, dogies, and move kinda slow,
   And don't be forever so much on the go,
   Move slow, little dogies, move slow. Hi-o, hi-o, hi-o.

2. Oh, lay down, my dogies, quit sifting around,
   Just stretch away out on the big, open ground.
   My horse is leg-weary and I'm awful tired,
   If you get away, then I'll surely be fired.
   Oh, lay down, my dogies, lay down. Hi-o, hi-o, hi-o.

The sun went down in a golden sky,
The lake was golden, too,
And now one silver star shines out
In a sky of velvet blue.

Go to Sleep, My Baby
(Arriba del cielo)

SPANISH-AMERICAN, from ARIZONA

Lull - a - by, lull - a - by,
Go to sleep, my ba - by, Good St. Anne is keep - ing
A - rri - ba del cie - lo, Está u - na ven - ta - na,
Lull - a - by, lull - a - by.
Watch a - bove your cra - dle, All the while you're sleep - ing.
Por don - de se a so - ma Se - ño - ra San - ta An - na.

Try to sing the Spanish words for this song.

Golden Slumbers

TRADITIONAL
FOLK SONG

1. Gold-en slum-bers kiss your eyes,
2. 'Neath each drow-sy, droop-ing lid

Smiles a-wait you when you rise;
Dreams from fair-y-land are hid;

1,2. Sleep, pret-ty loved one, do not cry,

And I will sing your lull-a-by.

Lull-a-by, lull-a-by,

Lull - a - by.

The sharps or flats at the beginning of a song are called *key signatures*. Notice that there are three sharps at the beginning of this song. They tell you that *do* is in the second space.

Pedro and the Goats

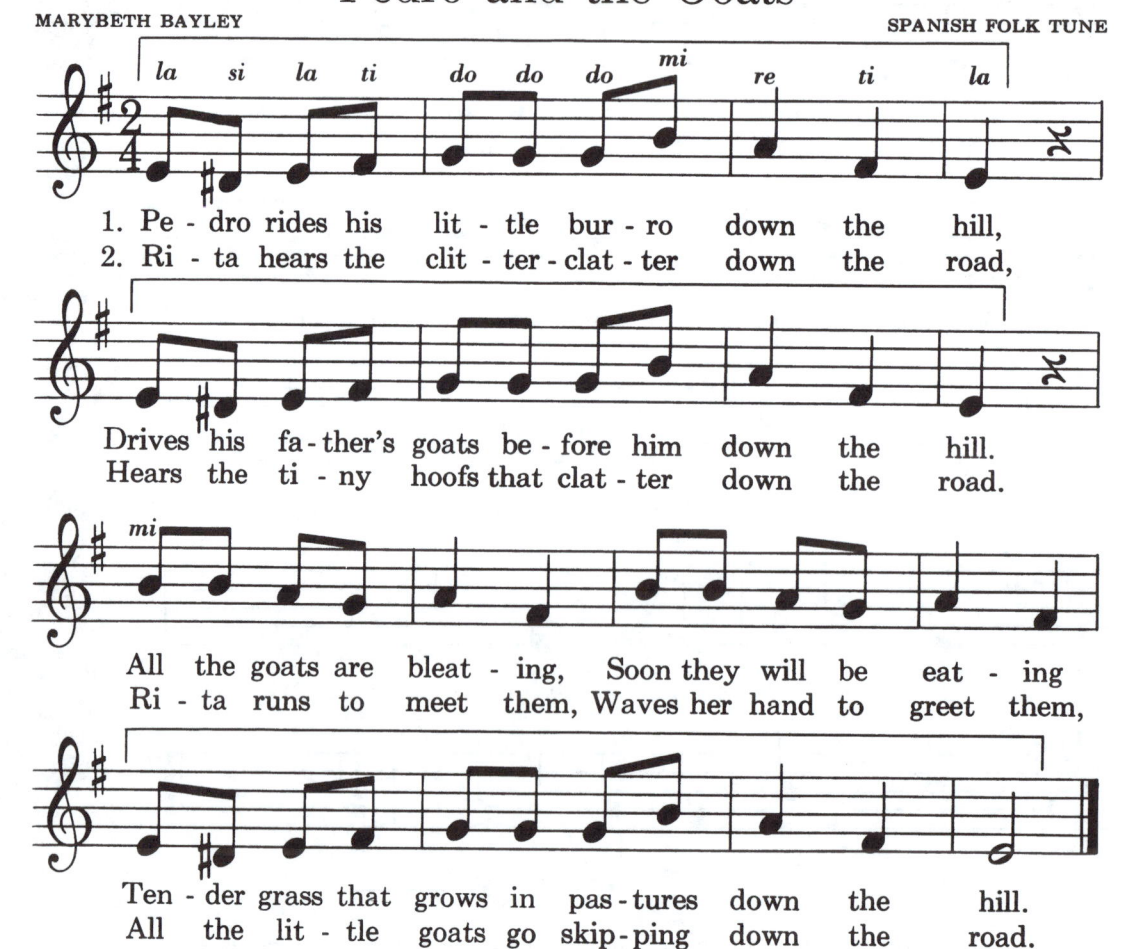

MARYBETH BAYLEY
SPANISH FOLK TUNE

la si la ti do do do mi re ti la

1. Pe - dro rides his lit - tle bur - ro down the hill,
2. Ri - ta hears the clit - ter - clat - ter down the road,

Drives his fa - ther's goats be - fore him down the hill.
Hears the ti - ny hoofs that clat - ter down the road.

mi

All the goats are bleat - ing, Soon they will be eat - ing
Ri - ta runs to meet them, Waves her hand to greet them,

Ten - der grass that grows in pas - tures down the hill.
All the lit - tle goats go skip - ping down the road.

When *so* has a sharp before it, it sounds a little higher and changes its name to *si*.

42

Let the people praise Thee, O God: let all the people praise Thee: the earth hath yielded her fruit.

Psalm 66

Sung at Harvest Time

English version by
CHRISTINE TURNER CURTIS

PERUVIAN INDIAN MELODY

1. Come, my sis-ters, come, my broth-ers, At the sound-ing of the horn;
2. Praise to Thee, O might-y Fa-ther, For the bar-ley and the cane!

On the hill-sides, on the moun-tains, Har-vest we the yel-low corn.
In the wheat fields, in the corn fields, Har-vest we the yel-low grain.

Gold-en shines our Broth-er Sun; Sil-ver shines our Sis-ter Moon;
Soft-ly blows the au-tumn wind; Gen-tly wave the silk-en leaves;

Sick-les flash-ing, fill your bas-kets, Reap-ing in the yel-low noon.
Reap-ers sing-ing, press we on-ward, Ty-ing up the yel-low sheaves.

How many times do you see this long rhythm pattern? (♩. ♪ ♫ ♫ ♩)
Clap it or play it on an Indian drum.

Canticle of Praise

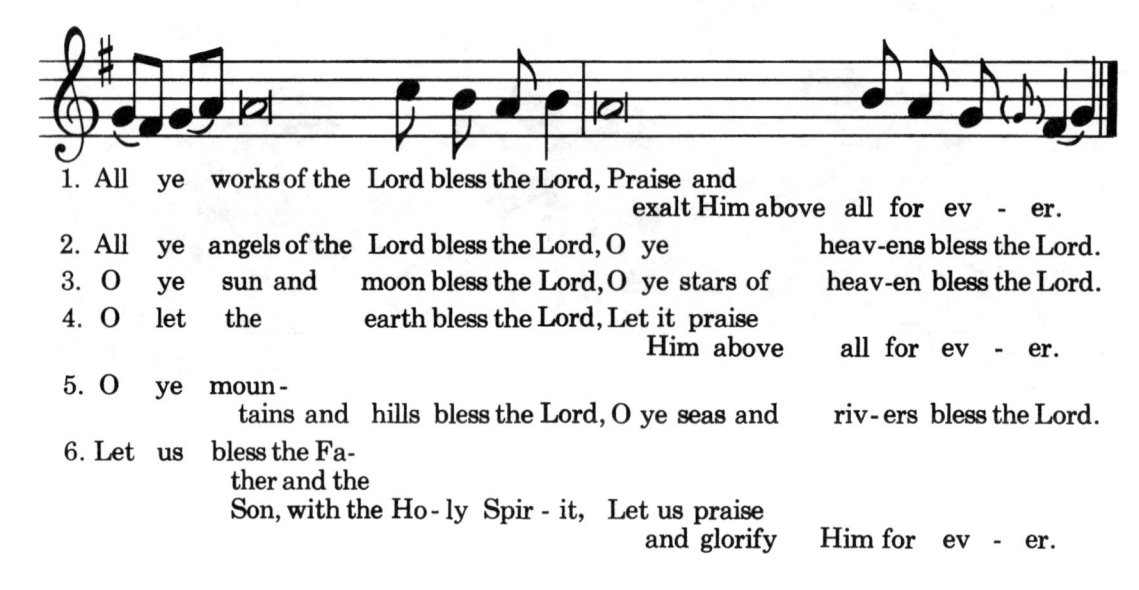

1. All ye works of the Lord bless the Lord, Praise and exalt Him above all for ev-er.
2. All ye angels of the Lord bless the Lord, O ye heav-ens bless the Lord.
3. O ye sun and moon bless the Lord, O ye stars of heav-en bless the Lord.
4. O let the earth bless the Lord, Let it praise Him above all for ev-er.
5. O ye moun-tains and hills bless the Lord, O ye seas and riv-ers bless the Lord.
6. Let us bless the Fa-ther and the Son, with the Ho-ly Spir-it, Let us praise and glorify Him for ev-er.

Thanksgiving Song

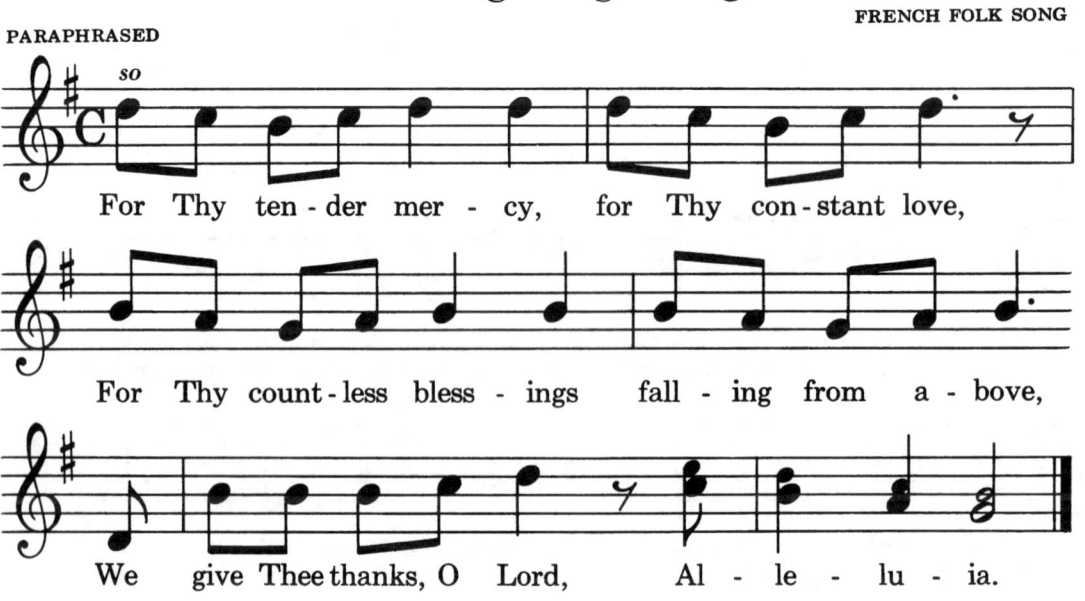

FRENCH FOLK SONG

PARAPHRASED

For Thy ten-der mer-cy, for Thy con-stant love,

For Thy count-less bless-ings fall-ing from a-bove,

We give Thee thanks, O Lord, Al-le-lu-ia.

The key signature for this song is one sharp. It tells you that *do* is on the second line.

Seek Ye the Lord

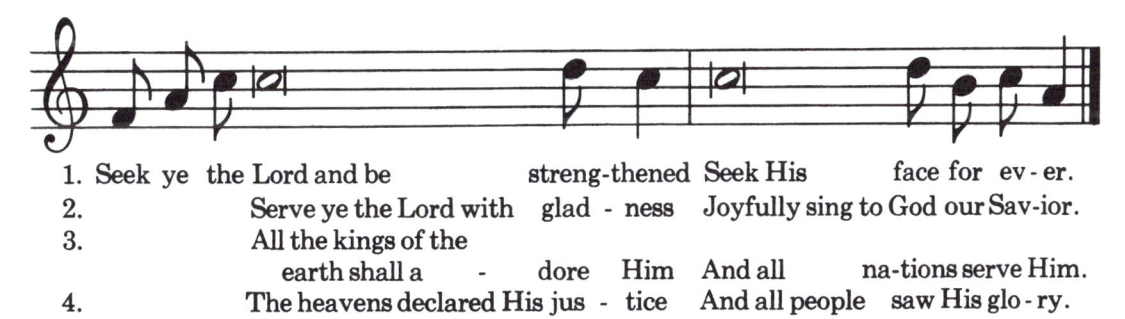

1. Seek ye the Lord and be strengthened Seek His face for ev-er.
2. Serve ye the Lord with glad-ness Joyfully sing to God our Sav-ior.
3. All the kings of the earth shall a-dore Him And all na-tions serve Him.
4. The heavens declared His jus-tice And all people saw His glo-ry.

Bless the Lord

SISTER CECILIA, S.C.
G. J. ELVEY

Bless the Lord and sound His praise, Glad and grate-ful voic-es raise,

Joy-ful be the hymn we sing Un-to our E-ter-nal King.

Bless His mer-cy, bless His love, Gra-cious gifts from heav'n a-bove!

Heav'n-ly Fa-ther, grant that we Thank-ful for Thy gifts may be!

Advent

Behold the Lord shall come, the Prince of the kings of the earth: blessed are they who are prepared to meet Him.

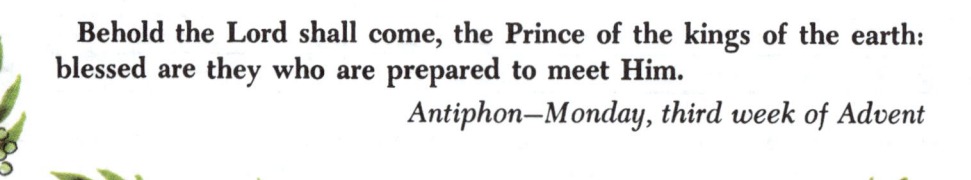

Antiphon—Monday, third week of Advent

O Come, O Come, Emmanuel

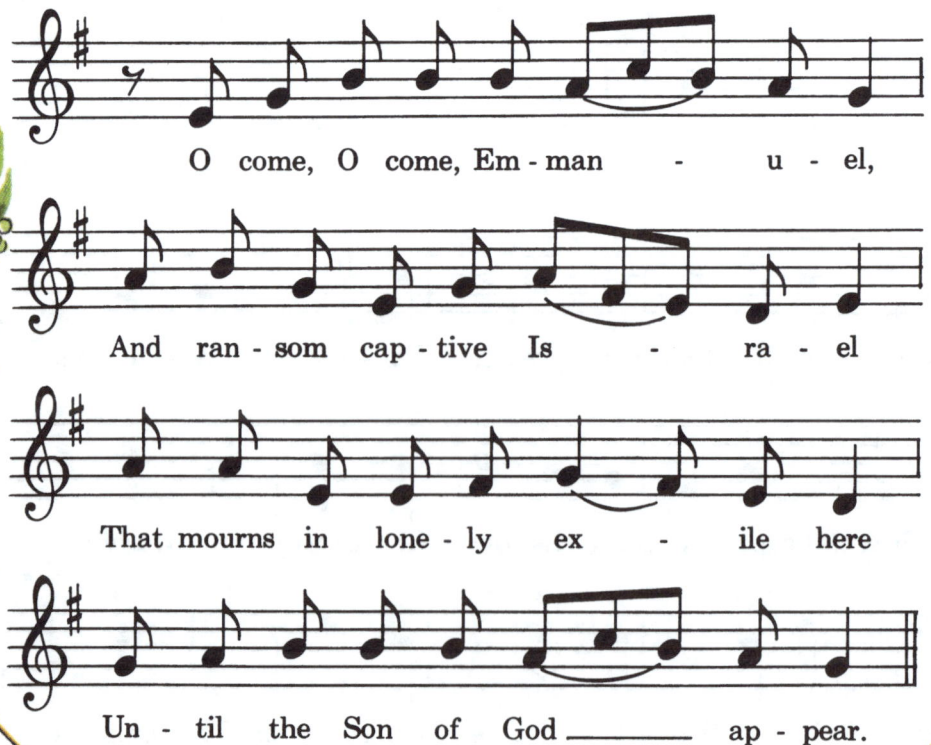

O come, O come, Em-man-u-el,

And ran-som cap-tive Is - ra-el

That mourns in lone-ly ex - ile here

Un-til the Son of God ____ ap-pear.

Re - joice! Re - joice! O Is - ra - el,
To thee shall come Em - man - u - el.

Soon Will the Christ Child Come

Translated by s. c.   FRENCH NOEL

la si la ti ti do do ti

1. Soon will the Christ Child come a - gain,
2. Dark was the road to Beth - le - hem,

so fa mi

Soon will the Babe be born a - new.
Cold was the cave that Christ - mas night.

Make Him a cra - dle in your heart,
Now, when the Christ Child comes to you,

Bid Him to come and dwell in you.
Give Him a wel - come warm and bright.

How often do you hear *la si la* in this song?

47

The Advent Wreath

SISTER CECILIA, S.C.

Fa - ther will light the first bright can - dle,

And Moth - er will light the next one.

Tom - my will light the third one,

Be - cause he is the old - est.

Mine is the last, my can-dle is wait-ing,

Just be-fore Christ-mas I shall be light-ing it.

Ma - ry, dear, it will shine for you,

On the way to Beth - le - hem.

The Jay Birds

MACRINA SOKOL FOLK TUNE

do so ti re so ti re fa mi

1. No-vem-ber days are chill-y and all the trees are bare,
2. The jay birds are so nois-y, the jay birds are so bold,

The jay birds steal the a-corns and hide them ev-'ry-where.
But oh, I like to see them when win-ter winds blow cold.

CHORUS

Ho! Ho! We'll have snow when No-vem-ber breez-es blow!

Jay birds, please don't go when No-vem-ber breez-es blow!

One sharp tells you that *do* is on the second line.
Sing the whole song with syllables before you sing the words.

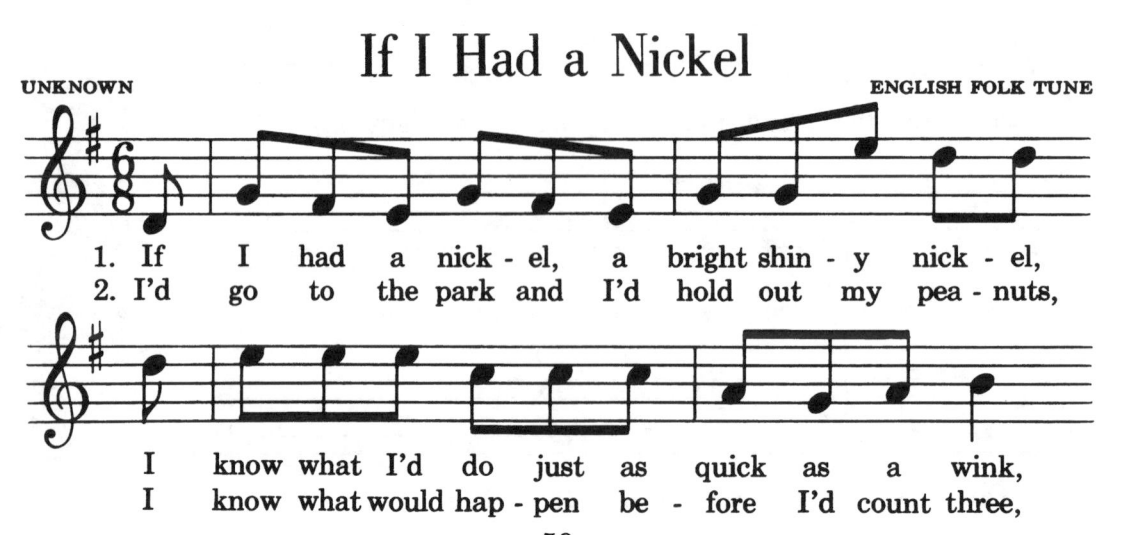

If I Had a Nickel

UNKNOWN ENGLISH FOLK TUNE

1. If I had a nick-el, a bright shin-y nick-el,
2. I'd go to the park and I'd hold out my pea-nuts,

I know what I'd do just as quick as a wink,
I know what would hap-pen be-fore I'd count three,

50

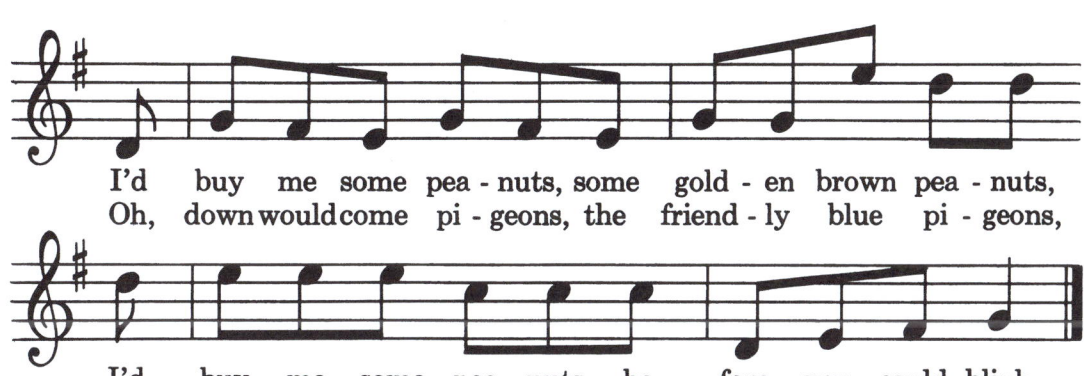

I'd buy me some pea-nuts, some gold-en brown pea-nuts,
Oh, down would come pi-geons, the friend-ly blue pi-geons,

I'd buy me some pea-nuts be-fore you could blink.
To eat up my pea-nuts and vis-it with me.

Are any phrases alike in this song?
Are any phrases almost alike?

Three Ponies

English version by ELEANOR FARJEON

DANISH FOLK SONG

1. What will you ride on? I'll ride a nut-brown po-ny;
2. What will you ride on? I'll ride a coal-black po-ny;
3. What will you ride on? I'll ride a snow-white po-ny;

re so   *so do mi*

Stur-dy hal-ter, i-ron bit, On his back a-stride I sit.
Scar-let sad-dle, silk-en reins, I will cross the des-ert plains.
Sil-ver bri-dle, gold-en girth, I will trav-el 'round the earth.

Hey, my nut-brown po-ny!
Hey, my coal-black po-ny!
Hey, my snow-white po-ny!

The time signature tells you that there are two beats in a measure. Tap these beats while you sing.

51

The Hunters

CLARINE KEEHN
GERMAN FOLK TUNE

We love the win-ter weath-er, The frost-y air, the winds that blow,

We love the win-ter snow, We love the win-ter snow.

A-hunt-ing we will go, will go, A-cross the fields and through the snow;

A-hunt-ing we will go, A-hunt-ing we will go.

*Hal-li, hal-lo, hal-li, hal-lo, A-hunt-ing we will go.

Hal-li, hal-lo, hal-li, hal-lo, A-hunt-ing we will go.

*Pronounce *hahl-lee*

Play on wood blocks for hoof beats.

Brother, Come and Dance

From "HANSEL AND GRETEL", HUMPERDINCK

GRETEL

Brother, come and dance with me, Both my hands I give to thee;
Right foot first, left foot then, Round a-bout and back a-gain.

HANSEL

I would dance, but don't know how, When to step and when to bow;
Show me what I ought to do And then I'll come and dance with you.

BOTH

Let your feet go tap, tap, tap, Let your hands go clap, clap, clap;
Let your head go nick, nick, nick, Let your fin-gers click, click, click;
Right foot first, left foot then, Round a-bout and back a-gain.
Right foot first, left foot then, Round a-bout and back a-gain.

This dance occurs in the opera *Hansel and Gretel.* You will enjoy hearing a recording of it.

The snow had begun in the gloaming
    And busily all the night
Had been heaping field and highway
    With a silence deep and white.

Every pine and fir and hemlock
    Wore ermine too dear for an earl,
And the poorest twig on the elm-tree
    Was ridged inch deep with pearl.
James Russell Lowell

The Snow

The snow covers the grass;
It covers the trees and it covers the houses.
Ev-'ry-thing now is white and love-ly
And beau-ti-ful.

Bye, Baby, Bye,

J. C. TYNDALL
SISTER ROSE MARGARET, C.S.J.

The sun has gone from the shin-y skies, Bye, ba-by, bye,—

The lambs have closed their sleep-y eyes, Bye, ba-by, bye,—

The stars are light-ing their lamps to see

If ba-bies and squirr'ls and the birds, all three,

Are sound a-sleep as they ought to be, Bye, ba-by, bye,—

How many tunes do you hear in this song?

Bye, ba-by, bye.—

Song before Christmas

English version by CECIL COWDREY

GERMAN FOLK SONG

1. Sing to-day a song of right good cheer.
2. Now's the time for keep-ing hol-i-day;

Sing, for Christ-mas Day will soon be here!
School doors close, and books are put a-way.

La la la la, mer-ry let us be.
La la la la, Christ-mas Day is near;

Soon we'll sing a-round the Christ-mas tree;
Good Saint Nich-o-las will soon be here;

Soon we'll sing a-round the Christ-mas tree;
Good Saint Nich-o-las will soon be here.

Remember to tap only once for two eighth notes.
Notice that there are three flats at the beginning of this song.
Where is *do*?

56

Christmas Is Coming

English version by **ROSE FYLEMAN**
POLISH FOLK SONG

do re ti do so

1. Christ-mas is com-ing; oh, the hap-py time!
2. Far in the for-est stands a lit-tle tree,
3. Christ-mas is com-ing; glad we are and gay.

Christ-mas is com-ing; sing a mer-ry rime.
Wait-ing and long-ing for the days to be,
Christ-mas is com-ing; sing a roun-de-lay.

fa re ti so

Tell me, what is Christ-mas bring-ing?
When it shall be bright and shin-ing,
Soon in spite of win-try weath-er,

Love and joy, and gay bells ring-ing
Gar-lands in its branch-es twin-ing,
All the world shall make to-geth-er

With a gold-en chime.
All for you and me.
Lov-ing hol-i-day.

Two flats in the key signature tell you that *do* is on the third line. Sing the song with syllables.

Tap two beats to each measure on a triangle.

Jingle Bells

J. PIERPONT

Dash-ing through the snow In a one-horse o-pen sleigh,

O'er the fields we go, Laugh-ing all the way;

Bells on bob-tail ring, Mak-ing spir-its bright;

What fun it is to ride and sing A sleigh-ing song to-night!

Chorus

Jin-gle bells! Jin-gle bells! Jin-gle all the way!

Oh, what fun it is to ride in a one-horse o-pen sleigh!

Jin - gle bells! Jin - gle bells! Jin - gle all the way!

Oh, what fun it is to ride in a one-horse o - pen sleigh!

You will enjoy accompanying the singing of this song with sleigh bells.

Stories of Travel

LOUISE AYRES GARNETT CZECHOSLOVAKIAN FOLK TUNE

1. Once I set out to dis - cov - er where the world ends,
2. Still I trav - eled on and on - ward; far did I go,

Down a riv - er, up a moun - tain, where the sky bends.
O - ver riv - ers, o - ver moun - tains, through the deep snow.

But the way, strange to say, ran a - long night and day;
All the way, day by day, did not stop, did not play,

Yet I nev - er could dis - cov - er where the world ends.
Till I found my home all shin - ing in the sun's glow.

Look at the time signature. How many beats will you tap in each measure?
How many eighth notes will you sing for each tap?
You will enjoy playing this tune on melody instruments.

O SALUTARIS HOSTIA

O saving Victim,
Who dost open the gate of heaven,
Wars with our enemies press upon us.
Give strength, bring help.

To the one and triune Lord,
Let eternal praise be given;
And may He grant us life without end
In our true native land. Amen.

St. Thomas Aquinas

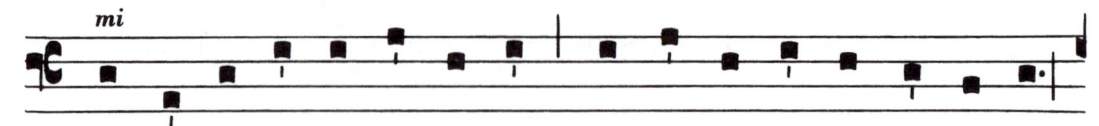

O Salutaris

O sa - lu - tá - ris Hó - sti - a, Quae cae - li pán - dis ó - sti - um,
U - ni tri - nó - que Dó - mi - no Sit sem - pi - tér - na gló - ri - a,

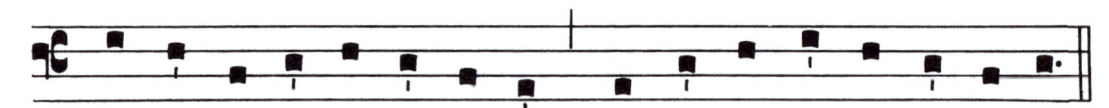

Bél - la pré - munt ho - stí - li - a, Da ró - bur, fer au - xí - li - um.
Qui ví - tam si - ne tér - mi - no Nó - bis dó - net in pá - tri - a.

This sign ▬ is a *fa clef*. It tells you that *fa* is on the third line. Where will you find *do*? Sing all of the hymn with syllables.

Protect Us, O Lord

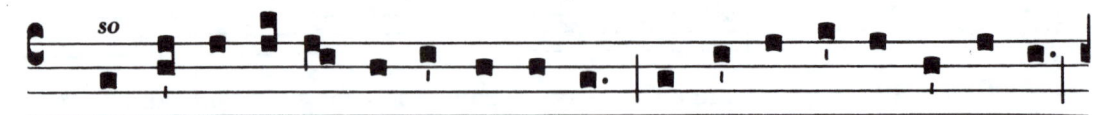

Pro - tect us, O Lord, while we are a - wake, and keep us while we are a - sleep:

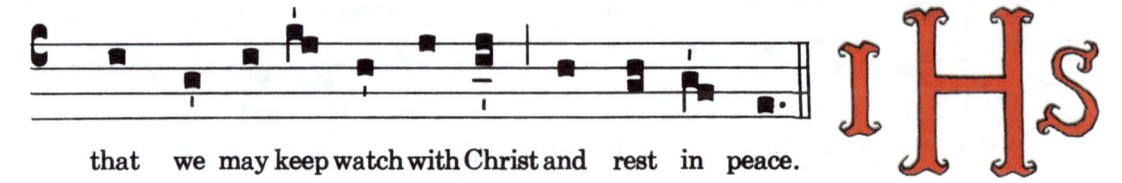

that we may keep watch with Christ and rest in peace.

Can you find more than one *podatus*? ▪ Can you find more than one *clivis*? ▪ Always sing lightly the second note of the *podatus* and the second note of the *clivis*.

Sanctus - Benedictus

Sán - ctus,* Sán - ctus, Sán - ctus Dó - mi - nus Dé - us
(*Holy, holy, holy, Lord God of*

Sá - ba - oth. Plé - ni sunt caé - li et tér - ra gló - ri - a tú - a.
Sabaoth.) (*Heaven and earth are full of Thy glory.*)

Ho - sán - na in ex - cél - sis. Bé - ne - dí - ctus qui
(*Hosanna in the highest.*) (*Blessed is he*

vé - nit in nó - mi - ne Dó - mi - ni. Ho-sán - na in ex - cél - sis.
that comes in the name of the Lord.) (*Hosanna in the highest.*)

Do you remember how to count a *dotted punctum*?

Christmastide and After

A little Child is this day born unto us, and He shall be called God, the Mighty One.

Antiphon—Christmas Day

Adeste Fideles

TRADITIONAL

1. Ad - é - ste fi - dé - les, Lae - ti tri - um - phán - tes
2. Can - tet nunc I - o Cho - rus An - ge - ló - rum;

Ve - ní - te, ve - ní - te in Béth - le - hem.
Can - tet nunc au - la cae - lé - sti - um.

Na - tum vi - dé - te Re - gem An - ge - ló - rum;
Gló - ri - a gló - ria In ex - cél - sis De - o:

1,2. Ve - ní - te ad - o - ré - mus, Ve - ní - te ad - o - ré - mus,

Ve - ní - te ad - o - ré - mus___ Dó - mi - num.

A Christmas Song

Simply—in a narrative style

HENRY M. HALVORSON

do mi do la   fa mi re do ti la

1. When Ma-ry came to Beth-le-hem from Naz-'reth far a-way,
2. Then Ma-ry smiled and said to him, "Good Jo-seph, don't be sad.

The lit-tle town was crowd-ed for it was the cen-sus day.
The hay is clean and smells so sweet, I'm sure we should be glad:

Though Jo-seph looked and looked a-round to find a place to stay,
For now the time has come for me to bear with-in this fold

la

Why, all that he could find was just a sta-ble with some hay.
Dear Je-sus, God's be-got-ten Son, as Ga-briel has fore-told."

64

Silent Night

Translated from the original by
FATHER JOSEPH MOHR

FRANZ GRUBER

1. Si - lent night! Ho - ly night! All is calm, all is bright
2. Si - lent night! Ho - ly night! Shep-herds quake at the sight,
3. Si - lent night! Ho - ly night! Son of God, love's pure light

Round yon Vir - gin Moth - er and Child!
Glo - ries stream __ from heav - en a - far,
Ra - diant beams __ from Thy ho - ly face,

Ho - ly In - fant, so ten - der and mild,
Heav'n - ly hosts __ sing Al - le - lu - ia;
With the dawn of re - deem - ing grace,

Sleep in heav-en-ly peace, __ Sleep __ in heav-en-ly peace. __
Christ, the Sav-iour, is born! __ Christ, __ the Sav-iour, is born! __
Je - sus, Lord, at Thy birth! __ Je - sus, Lord, at Thy birth! __

A Child Is Born in Bethlehem

1. A Child is born in Beth-le-hem, Al-le-lu-ia. Good ti-dings for Je-ru-sa-lem, Al-le-lu-ia, Al-le-lu-ia. *Chor:* We all re-joice and sing, For Christ is born, let all a-dore. Our gifts to Him we bring.

2. O come, a-dore, the an-gels sing, Al-le-lu-ia. And give our hearts to Christ, the King, Al-le-lu-ia, Al-le-lu-ia.

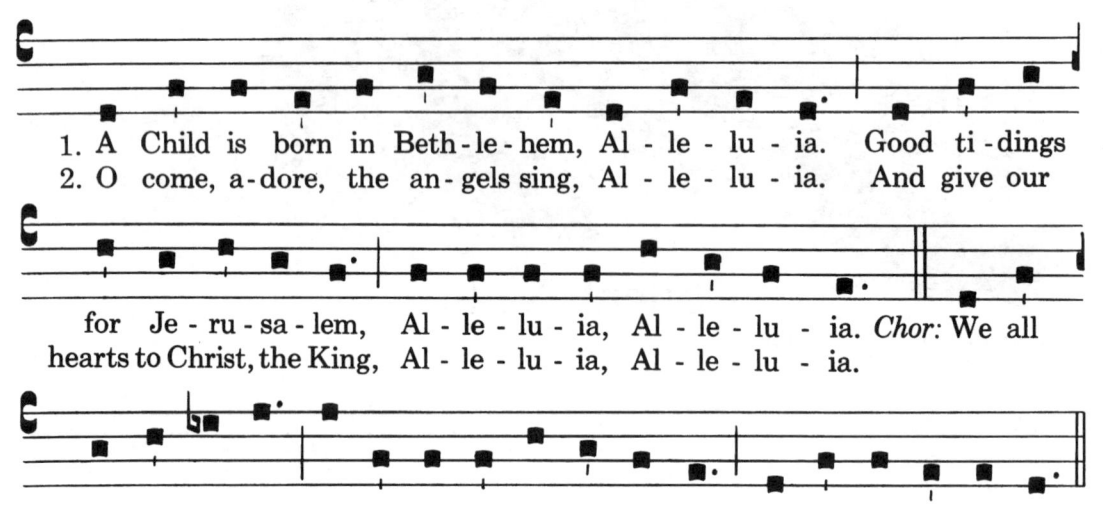

Lovely Infant

GERMAN CAROL

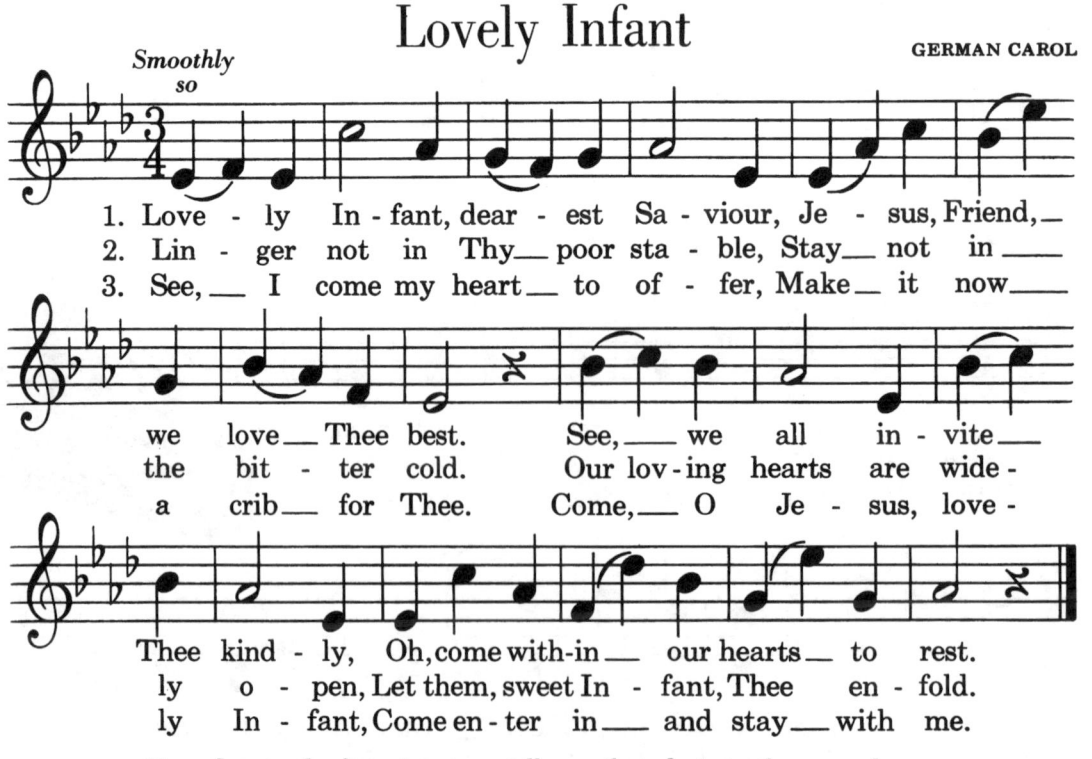

Smoothly

1. Love-ly In-fant, dear-est Sa-viour, Je-sus, Friend, so we love Thee best. See, we all in-vite Thee kind-ly, Oh, come with-in our hearts to rest.
2. Lin-ger not in Thy poor sta-ble, Stay not in the bit-ter cold. Our lov-ing hearts are wide-ly o-pen, Let them, sweet In-fant, Thee en-fold.
3. See, I come my heart to of-fer, Make it now a crib for Thee. Come, O Je-sus, love-ly In-fant, Come en-ter in and stay with me.

Four flats in the key signature tell you that *do* is in the second space.
Songs usually end on *do*. Does this song?

The Friendly Beasts

TWELFTH CENTURY CAROL

1. Jesus our brother, kind and good,
Was humbly born in a stable rude;
The friendly beasts around him stood,
Jesus our brother, kind and good.

2. "I," said the donkey, shaggy and brown,
"I carried His mother up hill and down;
I carried His mother to Bethlehem town.
I," said the donkey shaggy and brown.

3. "I," said the cow all white and red,
"I gave Him my manger for His bed,
I gave Him my hay to pillow His head.
I," said the cow all white and red.

4. "I," said the sheep with curly horn,
"I gave Him my wool for His blanket warm,
He wore my coat on Christmas morn.
I," said the sheep with curly horn.

5. "I," said the dove from the rafters high,
"I cooed Him to sleep that He should not cry,
We cooed Him to sleep, my mate and I.
I," said the dove from rafters high.

6. Thus every beast, by some good spell,
In the stable dark was glad to tell
Of the gift that he gave Emmanuel.
The gift that he gave Emmanuel.

Christmas Blessings

KATHERINE EDELMAN SISTER JOHN JOSEPH, C.S.J.

Blest be the man-ger that cra-dled His head:

Blest be the Wise Men, star-guid-ed, star-led:

Blest be the Car-pen-ter, faith-ful and strong;

Blest be the mu-sic of heav-en-ly song;

Blest be the shep-herds who came to a-dore Him;

Blest, dou-bly blest, be the Moth-er who bore Him.

Mary's Child Was Jesus
TRADITIONAL

so

Ma - ry's Child was Je - sus, the on - ly Son of God,

He came to her from Heav - en, all of the Ho - ly Ghost.

mi re ti do la so

And now He comes to us.

He is our lit - tle Broth - er, oh, let us love Him most.

The little Jesus came to town;
The wind blew up, the wind blew down;
Out in the street the wind was bold;
Now who would house Him from the cold?

Then opened wide a stable door,
Fair were the rushes on the floor;
The Ox put forth a hornèd head:
"Come, Little Lord, here make Thy bed."

Up rose the Sheep were folded near:
"Thou Lamb of God, come, enter here."
He entered there to rush and reed,
Who was the Lamb of God indeed.

The Little Jesus came to town;
With Ox and Sheep He laid Him down;
Peace to the byre, peace to the fold,
For that they housed Him from the cold!
        Lizette Woodworth Reese

Come to the Manger

SISTER JOHN JOSEPH, C.S.J.   CZECH FOLK TUNE

Joyfully

1. Come with us, oh hap-py chil-dren, We will has-ten to the man-ger,
2. We will kneel be-fore the man-ger, Bow in hum-ble ad-o-ra-tion.

We will greet the Ho-ly Child, the new-born In-fant Sav-iour.
He Who came to save the world is born this night in Beth-le-hem.

We will greet the Lit-tle One and Ma-ry and St. Jo-seph.
He, the One fore-told by proph-ets, He is born, the God-Man.

In how many measures do you find this rhythm pattern? (♩. ♪ ♩ ♩) Do you remember how it sounds?

Here Lies a Baby

Translated by JOHANNA C. F. AUER
Paraphrased by JANET TOBITT

NETHERLANDS CAROL

1. Here lies a Ba - by, O come and be - hold,
2. Young shep - herds, haste, to the sta - ble draw nigh,
3. Come, lit - tle an - gels, ap - proach to your King,

See how He's cry - ing and shiv - 'ring with cold,
Soothe the sweet Lamb with a soft lull - a - by,
Sure - ly He'll smile if a - round Him you sing,

See how He's cry - ing and shiv - 'ring with cold.
Soothe the sweet Lamb with a soft lull - a - by.
Sure - ly He'll smile if a - round Him you sing.

CHORUS

Na, na, na, na, na, na, sleep, my Ba - by, sleep,

Hush, hush, my Ba - by dear, please do not weep.

This song has many examples of the dotted quarter note followed by the eighth note.

Lullaby to the Infant Jesus

SALLY ANDERSON 　　　　　　　　　　　　　　　　　　　　　　MEXICAN CAROL

Oh, close your eyes, Dearest Infant Savior;

The stars are shining, O Sweetest Jesus.

The birds are silent now, no longer singing,

One of you can play this song on the piano while the others sing.

All na-ture's qui-et now and peace is bring-ing.

Then sleep till morn - ing, O In-fant Sav - ior,

The sun will wake You, O Sweet-est Je - sus.

Mexican songs often end on *mi* instead of *do*.

THE THREE KINGS
By Sister Cecilia, S.C.

This is the story of the three kings. It happened about two thousand years ago.

Imagine you are on a high hill in a country far away. It is a clear night and the stars are shining like diamonds. Three men are watching the stars. They are good men, and very wise. They are the three Magi, or the three kings; and they are watching for a sign in the heavens. They know that a great King is to be born into the world and a wonderful star will announce His birth. On this particular night the stars seem brighter than ever, when suddenly . . .

A bright new star sud-den-ly ap-pears,
A flam-ing star a-cross the mid-night.

The kings look at the star with amazement. They know it is the sign they have been waiting for. At last the Great King has been born. Immediately they call their servants to prepare the camels for a long journey. They will follow the wonderful star wherever it leads them. They know it will lead them to the birthplace of the Great King.

The kings are rid - ing o - ver the moun - tains

Fol - low - ing the beau - ti - ful __ star,

pp

Fol - low - ing the won - der - ful __ star,

Gleam - ing and glow - ing bright - er than a mil - lion oth - er stars, small - er stars.

A beau - ti - ful star light - ing all the heav - ens with its glo - ry.

Over mountains and hills and deserts the kings ride on their camels and always the wonderful star is bright in the western sky before them. They ride for many long weeks and sometimes grow very weary, but they never lose faith in their star. They know it will lead them to the birthplace of the Great King. And then, when they reach the city of Jerusalem ...

Sud-den-ly the star dis-ap-pears!

O - ver the roofs of Je - ru - sa - lem the star dis-ap-pears!

The kings are surprised. They look at one another with amazement. Nowhere in the sky can they find the flaming star.

Oh, where is our won-der-ful star? Oh, where is our beau-ti-ful star?

The kings are sad, the kings are sad.

Oh, how can they find their star?

The kings know that now they must ask for help. They ride to the palace of Herod, the king of Jerusalem, and ask him if he knows the birthplace of the Great King.

Herod is frightened. If a new king has been born will he take the kingdom away? The wicked king decides the Baby must be killed, but first the Baby must be found. So Herod asks his counselors if the prophecies tell where the Great King is to be born. And the counselors say . . .

Beth - le - hem, the cit - y of Da - vid,
Beth - le - hem, the cit - y of Da - vid,
Out of Da-vid's cit - y the King shall come.

Herod pretends to be glad. He says to the kings, "Go to Bethlehem and find the Child, and when you have found Him come and tell me so that I too may go and adore Him." But he really intends to have the Baby killed.

The three good kings do not suspect the wickedness of Herod. They promise to bring him news of the Child. So they set out for Bethlehem.

Down to Beth-le-hem now the car-a-van goes,

Hear the cam-el bells ring-ing, ting-a-ling-a-ling-ing,

Ring-ing, ting-a-ling-a-ling-ing,

Down the road to Beth-le-hem the car-a-van is swing-ing.

The gates of Jerusalem slowly close behind the caravan and the sky grows darker. A strange brightness begins to shine in the darkness, and then the star appears. It seems more beautiful than ever as it leads the way to Bethlehem. The kings ride silently through the night, their eyes lifted to the star. Now they know the end of the journey is near, and their hearts are glad.

They enter the city of Bethlehem. Now the star no longer moves before them. It stands still over the roof that shelters the newborn King. The three kings get down from their camels. Softly they go into the house. And there they find the Child in the arms of Mary, His mother.

Kneel-ing down they a-dore Him, Kneel-ing down they a-dore Him,

O-pen-ing their treas-ures they give to Him

Won-der-ful things, beau-ti-ful things, pre-cious things.

Gold is the gift of the first king, a casket of precious gold.

Gold I bring for a King,   Gold I bring for a King,
He is King of the whole world, He is King of my heart.

Incense is the gift of the second king, a box of priceless incense.

Frank - in - cense   I   bring to Christ, Our Lord,
He   is God, the Mak - er   of   the world.

In-cense with our prayer as-cend-ing to His throne,

Brings a shower of bless-ings from His hands.

Myrrh is the gift of the third king, a vase of costly perfume.

Myrrh is the gift I bring, Cost-ly and sweet per-fume,

For a Child Who will grow to be a Man,

For a Man Who will die some day, Myrrh shall em-balm Him in the tomb.

The kings would like to stay forever with the Holy Child, but they know they must carry the news of His birth to their own people. So they prepare to leave Bethlehem. Then a message comes to them from heaven that they must not return to Jerusalem. They must not tell the wicked Herod where he can find the Infant King. They must go back another way to their own country. Quietly they take leave of the Child and His mother. Soon they are far away.

Not too fast

Far a-way, the kings are far a-way, Far a-way, the kings are far a-way; Soft-er sound the tin-kling bells, Soft-er, soft-er, far a-way, far a-way.

At last they reach their own country. Everywhere, they tell the story of the King of Kings, born in a stable at Bethlehem. They tell the people that this Child is God, the Maker of heaven and earth. Their love for Jesus burns in their hearts forever, brighter than the wonderful star. One day, they know, they will find Him again in heaven. Then they will love and adore Him forever.

Je-sus born in Beth-le-hem, Kneel-ing we a-dore, All our love we give to Thee, Now and ev-er-more.

The End

Step Softly, Little Donkey

SPANISH FOLK TUNE, arranged

Lightly

la — re do ti si la

1. Step soft-ly, lit-tle don-key, With your pre-cious load,
2. Step soft-ly, lit-tle don-key, With God's lit-tle Son,
3. Step quick-ly, lit-tle don-key, Through the dark, dark night,

Her-od must not hear you, Go-ing down the road.
Do not wake the Ba-by, Lit-tle Ho-ly One,
You must be far, far a-way, Long be-fore it's light.

Chorus *faster*

Step soft-ly, lit-tle don-key, Step soft-ly, lit-tle don-key,

slower

Step soft-ly, lit-tle don-key, Go-ing down the road.

83

New Year

ENGLISH TERM PLAN   **ENGLISH FOLK TUNE**

Bells: Ding, dong, ding, dong, Ding, dong, ding, dong,

1. I am the New Year, ho, ho, ho! I come danc-ing o'er the snow,
2. Bless-ings I bring you, one and all, Big folks, small folks, short and tall.

Ding, dong, ding, dong, ding, dong, ding, dong.

Hear my bells ring, ding, ding, ding! So o-pen your doors and let me in.
Man-y treas-ures you may win, So o-pen your doors and let me in.

A key signature of one flat tells you that *do* is in the first space.

Reuben and Rachel

HARRY BIRCH WILLIAM GOOCH

Girls

1. Reu-ben, Reu-ben, I've been think-ing, What a queer world this would be
2. Reu-ben, Reu-ben, I've been think-ing, Life would be so eas-y then;
3. Reu-ben, Reu-ben, I've been think-ing, If we went be-yond the seas,

If the men were all trans-port-ed Far be-yond the North-ern Sea!
What a love-ly world this would be If there were no tire-some men!
All the men would fol-low aft-er Like a swarm of bum-ble-bees!

Boys

Ra-chel, Ra-chel, I've been think-ing, What a queer world this would be
Ra-chel, Ra-chel, I've been think-ing, Life would be so eas-y then;
Ra-chel, Ra-chel, I've been think-ing, If we went be-yond the seas,

If the girls were all trans-port-ed Far be-yond the North-ern Sea.
What a love-ly world this would be If you'd leave it to the men.
All the girls would fol-low aft-er Like a swarm of hon-ey-bees.

What does the top number in the time signature tell you?

The Skaters

CHRISTINE TURNER CURTIS　　　　　　　　　　　　　　　　　EMIL WALDTEUFEL

One swing to a measure

Skat - ers, a - way! Glide, glide and sway,
Skat - ers, fly on, Light as the swan.

Dart - ing and fly - ing like gulls at play. *Fine*
Skate till the pale win - ter sun is gone. gone.

On your sil - ver - y skates you go swirl - ing, swirl - ing,

O - ver the ice mad - ly whirl - ing, whirl - ing,

86

Scarves in the breez-es un-furl - ing, furl - ing,

Clink, ting-a-ling, a - ling, ting-a-ling, a - ling, ling.

On your sil-ver-y blades you go swirl - ing, swirl - ing,

Like diz-zy tops that are twirl - ing, twirl - ing.

Fast-er and fast-er you dash in your mer-ry chase

D.C. al Fine

All through the short win-ter day.

Jesu dulcis memoria

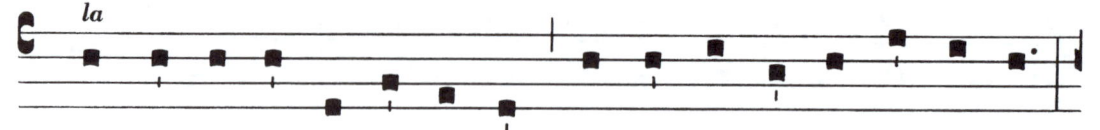

Jé - su dúl - cis me - mó - ri - a, Dans vé - ra cór - dis gáu - di - a:

Sed sú - per mel et óm - ni - a, E - jus dúl - cis prae - sén - ti - a.

This neum is a *climacus*. All notes in Gregorian Chant have one count. It does not matter whether they are square or diamond-shaped. How many counts has a *dotted punctum*?

Below is the same melody with English words.

O Jesus, Lord, Thy Holy Name

1. O Je - sus, Lord, Thy Ho - ly Name My com - fort and my joy will be,
2. O Je - sus, keep me pure and good, My lips and tongue I give to Thee,

Thou art my Sav - ior and my God,— And Thou didst die for love of me.
Oh, may they al - ways bless Thy Name,— And sing Thy praise e - ter - nal - ly.

Morning Hymn

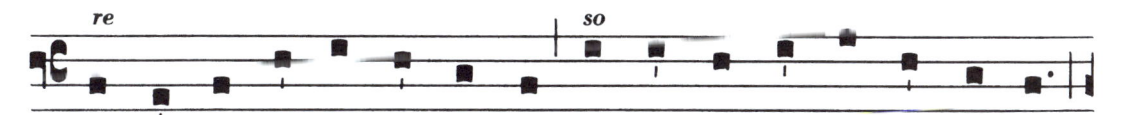

re   *so*

1. Now that the day-light fills the sky, We lift our hearts to God on high,
2. All praise to God the Fa - ther be, All praise, e - ter - nal Son, to Thee,

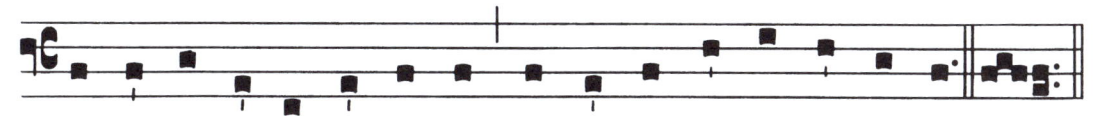

That He in all we do or say, Would keep us free from harm to - day.
All glo - ry as is ev - er meet, To God the Ho - ly Par - a - clete. A - men.

On the first syllable of the "Amen" we sing three notes ⬛, the second of which is the highest. This is called a *torculus* and the highest note is always sung lightly.

Notice that each note of the *podatus* ⬛: in the "Amen" has a dot after it. Give each dotted note two counts.

Evening Hymn

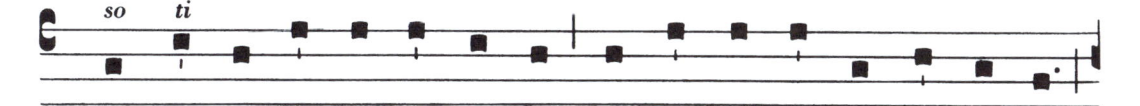

so   *ti*

1. Be - fore the end - ing of the day, Cre - a - tor of the world, we pray
2. O Fa - ther, grant that this be done Through Je - sus Christ, Thine on - ly Son,

That with Thy gra - cious fa - vor Thou Wouldst be our Guard and Keep - er now.
Who with the Ho - ly Ghost and Thee Shall live and reign e - ter - nal - ly. A - men.

Most of the time the Amen in chant is sung with a *torculus* and a *dotted podatus*.

Gently the Snow Is Falling

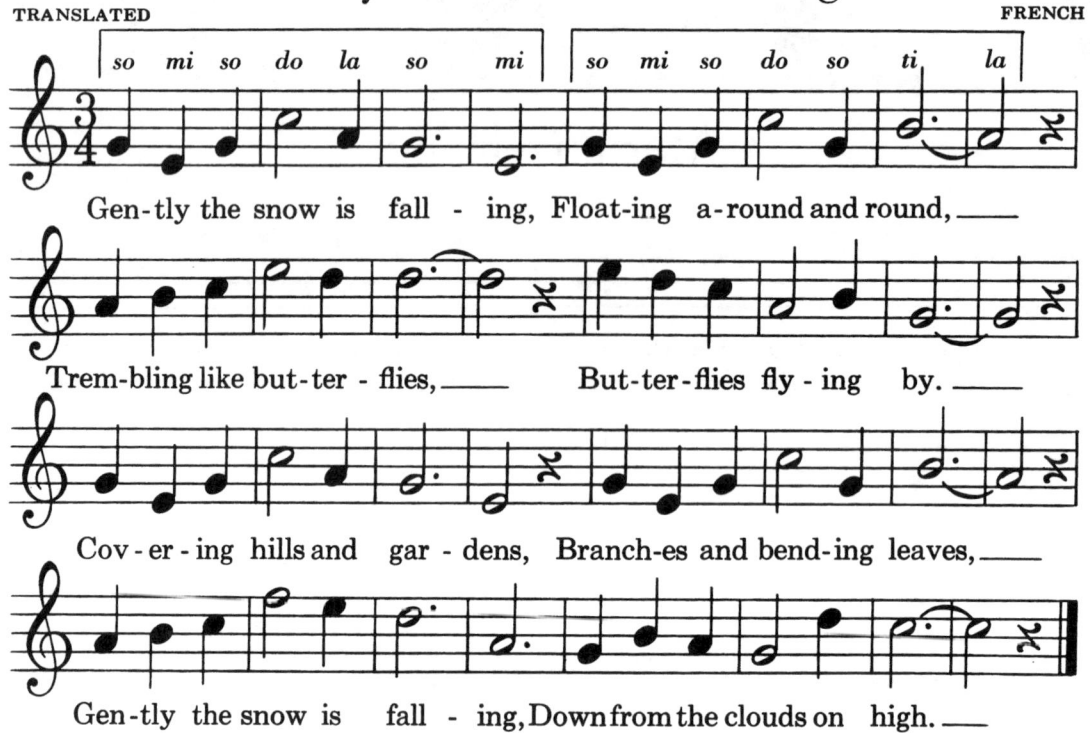

TRANSLATED FRENCH

so mi so do la so mi | so mi so do so ti la

Gen-tly the snow is fall-ing, Float-ing a-round and round,
Trem-bling like but-ter-flies, But-ter-flies fly-ing by.
Cov-er-ing hills and gar-dens, Branch-es and bend-ing leaves,
Gen-tly the snow is fall-ing, Down from the clouds on high.

What does the time signature tell you about this song?

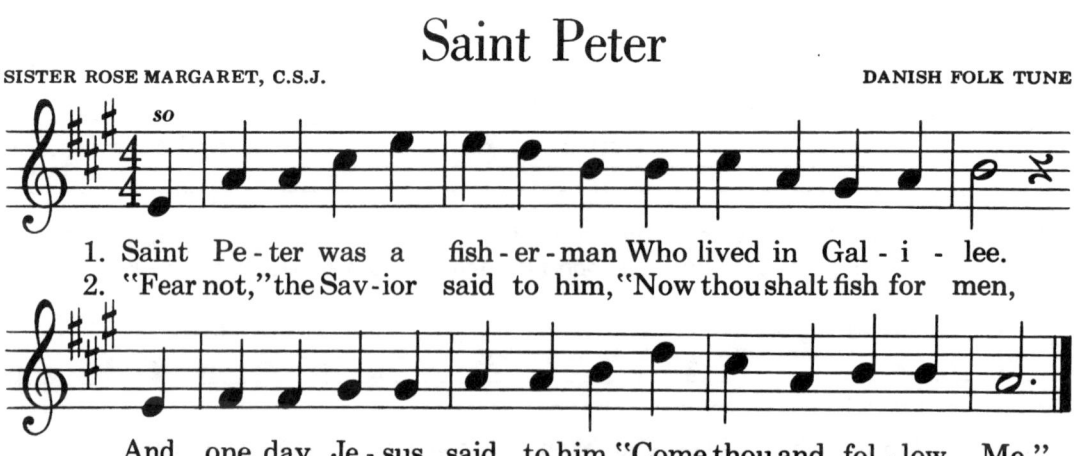

Saint Peter

SISTER ROSE MARGARET, C.S.J. DANISH FOLK TUNE

so

1. Saint Pe-ter was a fish-er-man Who lived in Gal-i-lee.
2. "Fear not," the Sav-ior said to him, "Now thou shalt fish for men,

And one day Je-sus said to him, "Come thou and fol-low Me."
And on this rock I'll build my Church, To live un-to the end."

Where is *do* when the key signature has three sharps?
How many beats do you give to each measure? How do you know?

Prayer for a Little Child

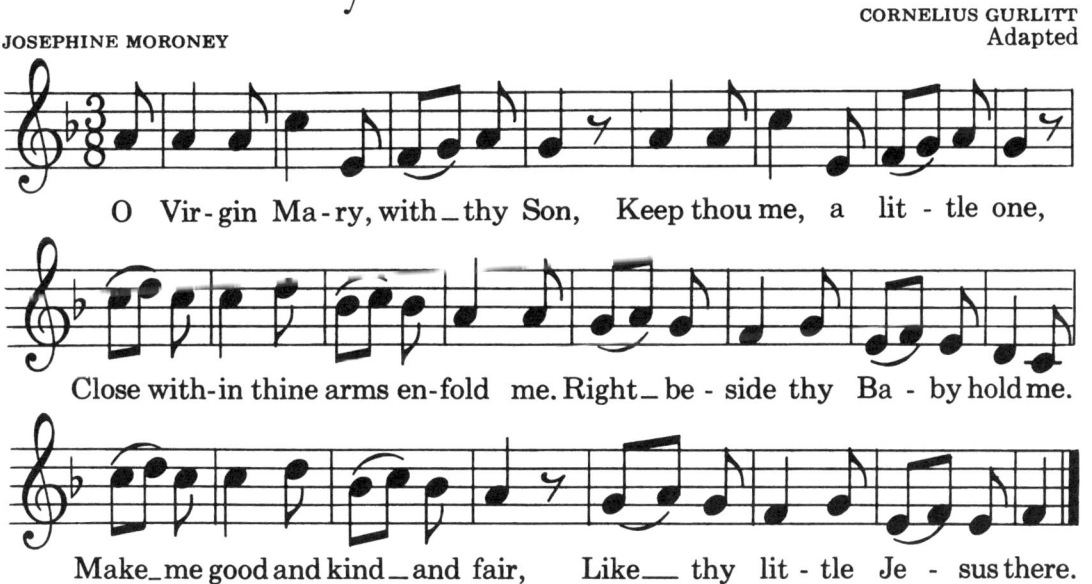

JOSEPHINE MORONEY

CORNELIUS GURLITT
Adapted

O Virgin Mary, with thy Son, Keep thou me, a little one,

Close within thine arms enfold me. Right beside thy Baby hold me.

Make me good and kind and fair, Like thy little Jesus there.

Which phrases are almost alike? Where are they different?

On the Road to Damascus

MARY WARD

1. On the road to Damascus, Who rides so wildly?
2. On the road to Damascus, Who calls the rider?

Saul, Saul, Burning with hatred for all the Christians,
"Saul, Saul, Why do you persecute Me, your Savior?"

Saul, Saul, Eager to put them all to death.
"Saul, Saul!" It is the voice of Christ, the Lord!

Do you know the rest of the story about Saul?

91

The Schooner Sally

SEA CHANTEY

1. 'Twas a cold and frost-y morn-ing,___ A-way, boys,__ a-way!
2. There was ice up-on her rig-ging,___ A-way, boys,__ a-way!
3. And her crew were all a-sing-ing,___ A-way, boys,__ a-way!
4. For her hold was full of her-ring,___ A-way, boys,__ a-way!

1-4. When we brought the schoon-er Sal-ly___ To Glouces-ter Bay.___

We Built a Snowman in the Yard

TRANSLATED

DUTCH FOLK SONG

1. We built a snow-man in the yard And he was fine to see,___
2. This morn-ing when we went to school Our snow-man stayed at home.___

And though he had-n't an-y toes, He had a splen-did car-rot nose.
When we came back he had a hat; Our dad-dy must have thought of that.

Ho ho ho,___ The spar-rows came to eat that nose!
Ho ho ho,___ The spar-rows sat up-on his hat!

Ho ho ho,___ We chased them all a-way.___
Ho ho ho,___ We chased them all a-way.___

Haul Away, Joe

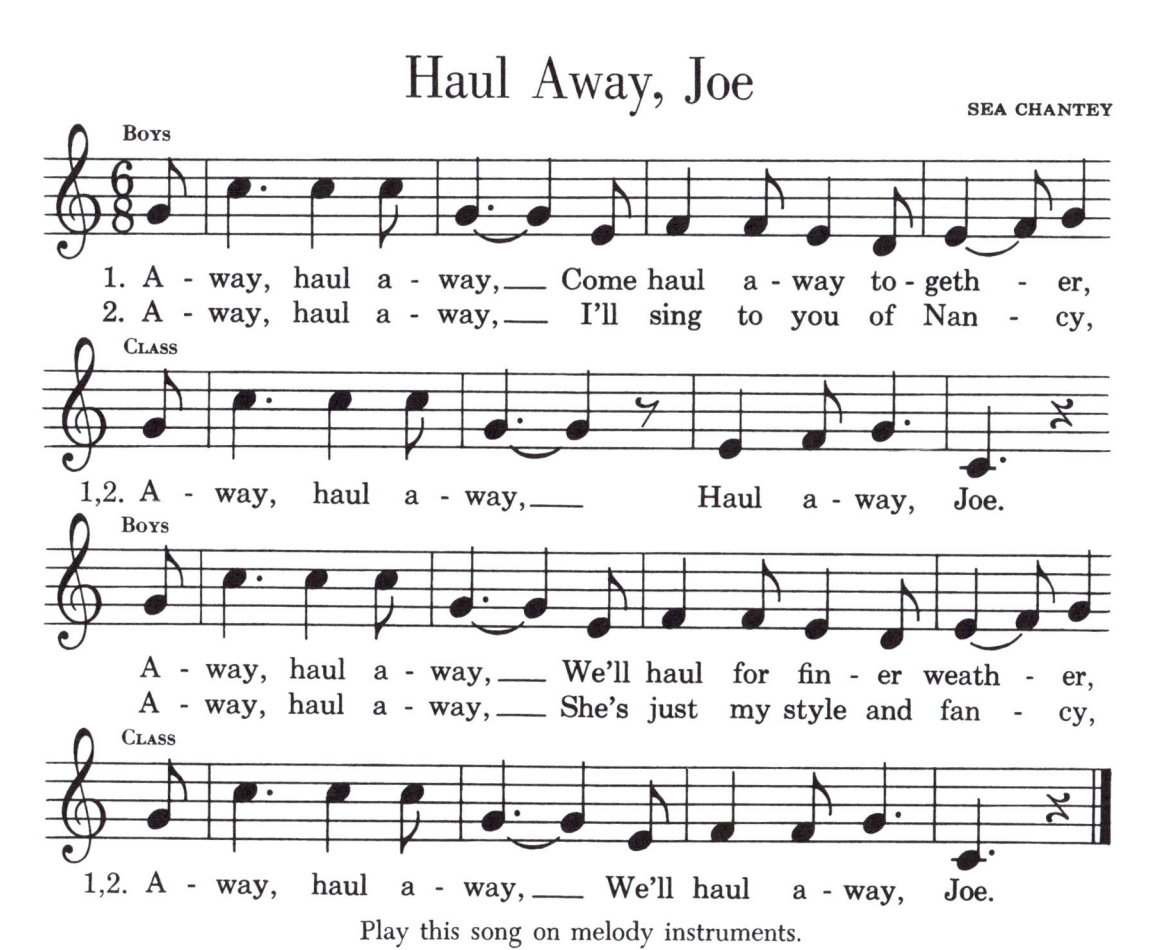

SEA CHANTEY

1. A-way, haul a-way,— Come haul a-way to-geth-er,
2. A-way, haul a-way,— I'll sing to you of Nan-cy,

1,2. A-way, haul a-way,— Haul a-way, Joe.

A-way, haul a-way,— We'll haul for fin-er weath-er,
A-way, haul a-way,— She's just my style and fan-cy,

1,2. A-way, haul a-way,— We'll haul a-way, Joe.

Play this song on melody instruments.

Our Lady's Lullaby

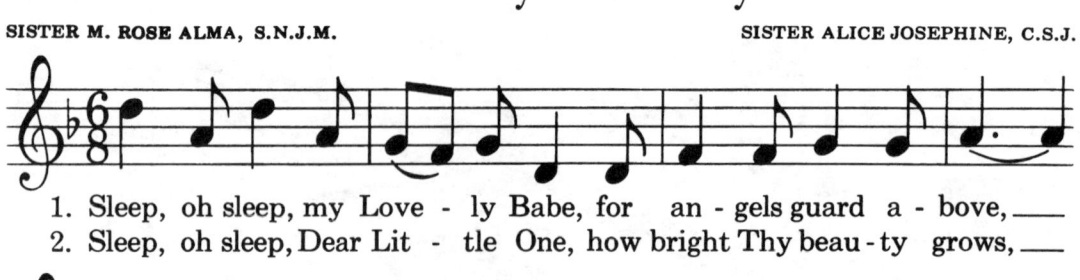

SISTER M. ROSE ALMA, S.N.J.M. SISTER ALICE JOSEPHINE, C.S.J.

1. Sleep, oh sleep, my Love-ly Babe, for an-gels guard a-bove,___
2. Sleep, oh sleep, Dear Lit-tle One, how bright Thy beau-ty grows,___

And Jo-seph, too, doth watch,___ with ten-der-ness and love.___
Oh sleep,___ my King, my God,___ for here love holds Thee close.___

Our Lady's Children

SISTER CECILIA, S.C.

Lit-tle girl from Mex-i-co, Lit-tle boy from Bor-ne-o,

Lit-tle girl from far Ma-lay, Lit-tle boy from U. S. A.,

Boys from Chi-na and Ja-pan, Girls from Spain and Switz-er-land,

Boys and girls from far and near Love Our Bless-ed Moth-er dear.

A Valentine Surprise

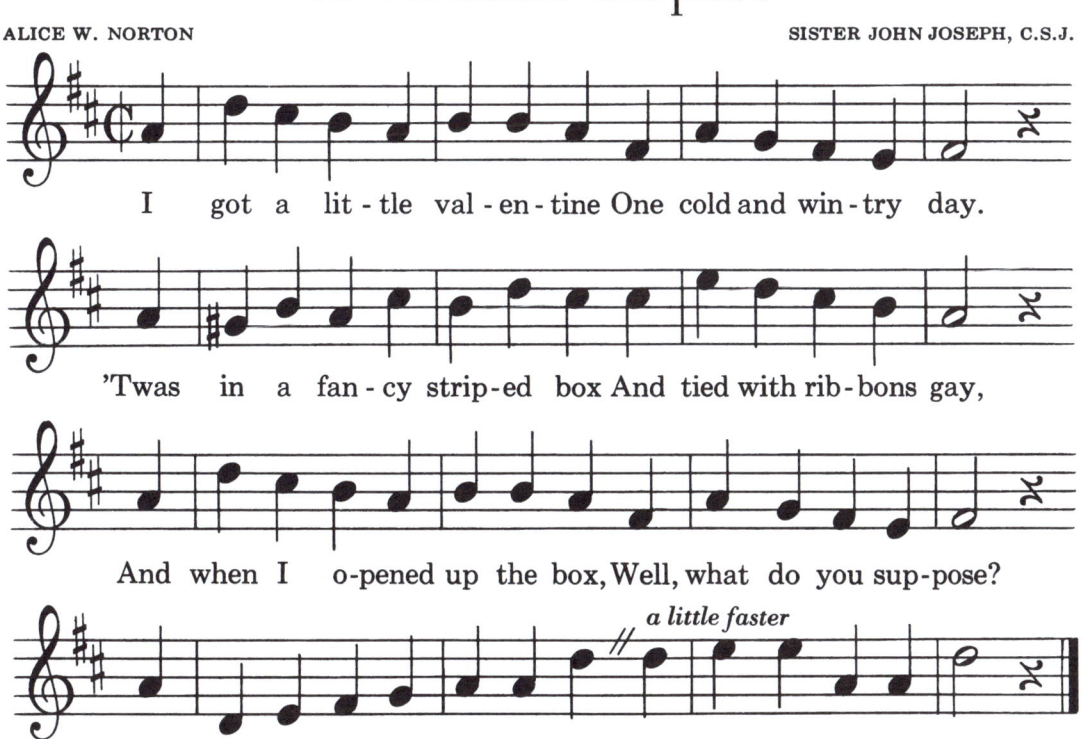

ALICE W. NORTON
SISTER JOHN JOSEPH, C.S.J.

I got a lit-tle val-en-tine One cold and win-try day.

'Twas in a fan-cy strip-ed box And tied with rib-bons gay,

And when I o-pened up the box, Well, what do you sup-pose?

a little faster

A live-ly pup-py dog jumped out And kissed me on the nose.

Our Country

JULIA DERLETH

CORNELIUS GURLITT
Adapted

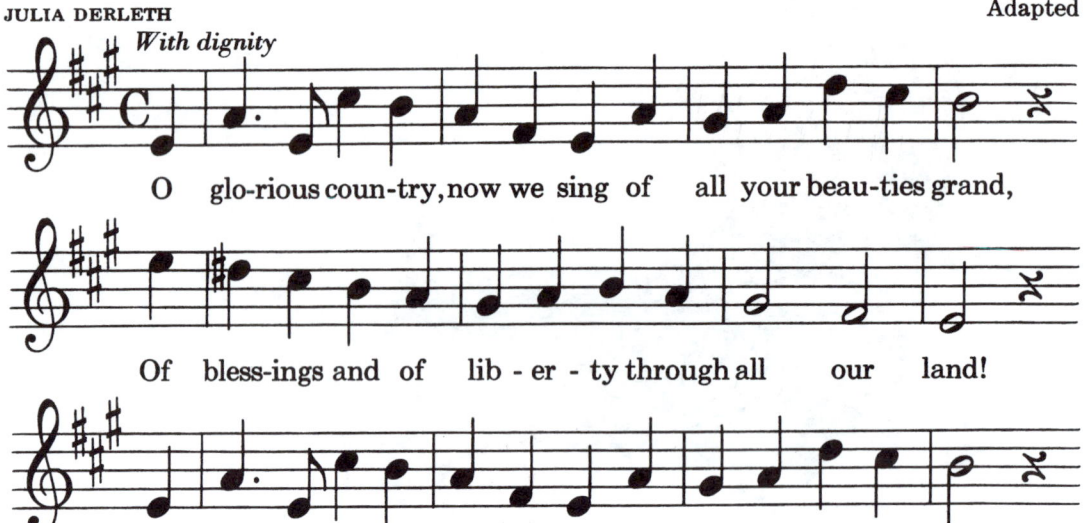

With dignity

O glo-rious coun-try, now we sing of all your beau-ties grand,

Of bless-ings and of lib-er-ty through all our land!

We're proud of you, your trust in God, your hope and cour-age great.

We love you, A-mer-i-ca, we love you, A-mer-i-ca, our glo-rious land.

The time signature C tells you that there are four beats in a measure.

Yankee Doodle

DR. SHACKBURG TRADITIONAL

1. Fath'r and I went down to camp A-long with Cap-tain Good-win,
2. There we saw a thou-sand men As rich as Squire David,
3. There was Cap-tain Wash-ing-ton Up-on a slap-ping stal-lion,

And there we saw the men and boys As thick as hast-y pud-din'.
And what they wast-ed ev-'ry day, I wish it could be sav-ed.
A-giv-ing or-ders to his men; I guess there was a mil-lion.

Chorus

Yan-kee Doo-dle, keep it up, Yan-kee Doo-dle dan-dy,

Mind the mu-sic and the step, And with the girls be hand-y.

Under the Snow

SISTER CECILIA, S.C.   MARK NOLAN

Un - der the snow, un - der the snow,
Green and ten - der the grass - es grow,
la la te la la so mi do
Wait - ing till skies with A - pril glow,
And gen - tle breez - es blow.____

When there is a flat (♭) before the note *ti*, it sounds a little lower, and its name is changed to *te*.

Falling Snow

CHRISTINE TURNER CURTIS
PAUL FORDE

1. Fall-ing snow, feath-er-y snow,
2. Fall-ing snow, sil-ver-y snow,

White as the down of swans,___
Flies on a drow-sy wing,___

Fall-ing so dream-i-ly, float-ing so la-zi-ly
Light as a but-ter-fly, hum-ming a lull-a-by

O-ver the fields and the lawns.___
O-ver the cra-dle of spring.___

Notice the *la-te-te-la* in this song.
How many times do you sing the rhythm pattern ♩. ♪ ♪?

FRANZ JOSEPH HAYDN

Franz Joseph Haydn was born March 31, 1732 in Austria. Because he had such a beautiful voice he was asked to sing in the church choir when he was still very young. He loved music so much that he wanted to study it and to compose songs for the other children to sing. Since his parents were very poor they could not afford to give him music lessons. He surprised everyone by teaching himself to play the piano.

Because of his great love for music and the great talent God gave him, he became one of the greatest composers of his time. Beethoven and Mozart, who also became famous musicians, were his pupils.

Haydn, a devout Catholic, was a very kind, happy, and humble man. He was called "Papa Haydn" by those who knew and loved him. His music is cheerful and bright.

Thanks to Our God

SISTER JOHN JOSEPH, C.S.J.

FRANZ JOSEPH HAYDN
Theme from SYMPHONY NO. 2

Thanks to our God for all His mer-cy and com-pas-sion.

Glo-ry, glo-ry, and ad-o-ra-tion give to Him.

Praise to our God, with ev-er-last-ing love and hon-or.

Blest for-ev-er____ be His name!

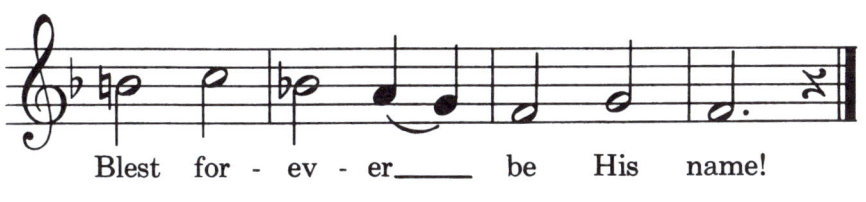

Country Dance

FRANZ JOSEPH HAYDN

This is one of Haydn's shortest pieces for the piano. How many of you can play it?

A New Created World · From "The Creation"

FRANZ JOSEPH HAYDN
Arranged

A new cre-a-ted world, a new cre-a-ted world
Springs up, springs up at God's com-mand, springs up at
God's com-mand, springs up at God's com-mand.

The Heavens Are Telling · From "The Creation"

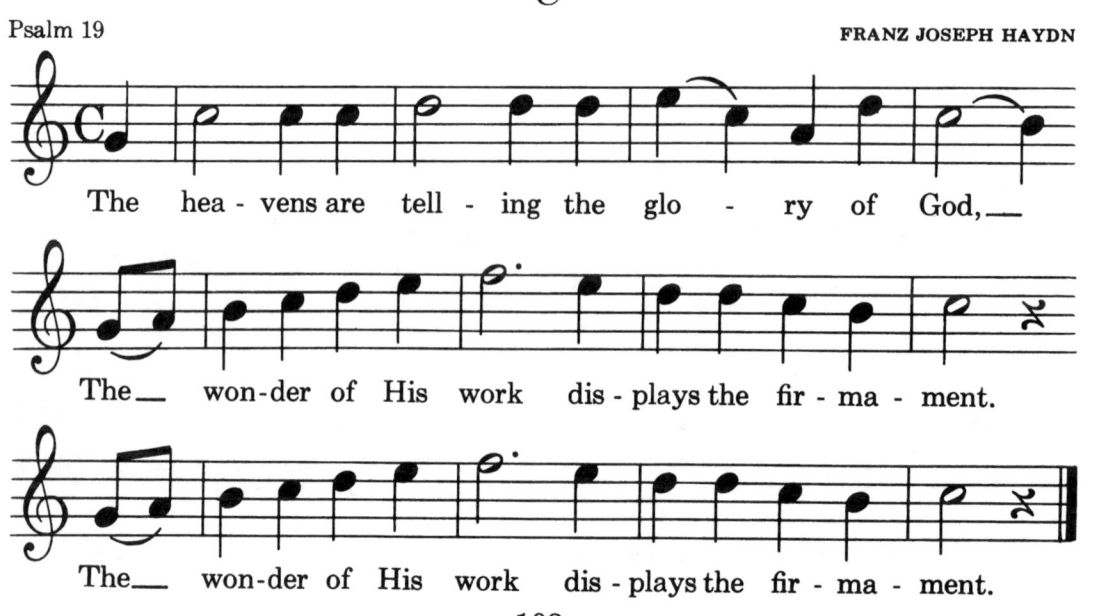

Psalm 19

FRANZ JOSEPH HAYDN

The hea-vens are tell-ing the glo-ry of God,
The won-der of His work dis-plays the fir-ma-ment.
The won-der of His work dis-plays the fir-ma-ment.

Lent and Passiontide

There are come to us days of penance, to redeem our sins and to save our souls.

Antiphon—first week of Lent

Stabat Mater

STÁ - bat Má - ter do - lo - ró - sa   Júx - ta crú - cem la - cri - mó - sa,
At   the Cross, her sta - tion keep - ing, Stood the mourn - ful Moth - er weep - ing,

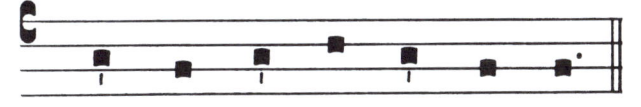

Dum pen - dé - bat Fí - li - us.
Close to Je - sus to the last.

In Gregorian Chant a flat looks like this. (♭) This flat sign tells you to sing *te* instead of *ti*. It will sound lower than *ti*.

Parce Domine

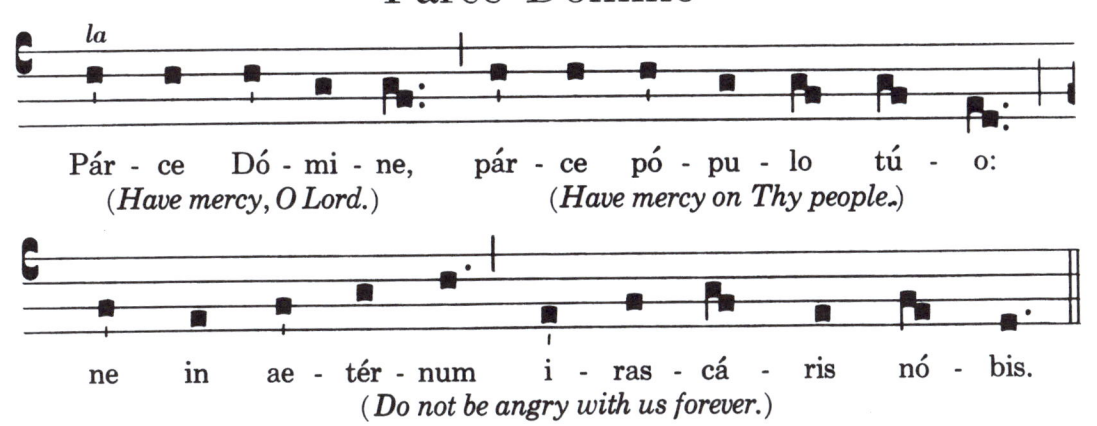

Pár - ce Dó - mi - ne,   pár - ce pó - pu - lo tú - o:
(Have mercy, O Lord.)   (Have mercy on Thy people.)

ne in ae - tér - num i - ras - cá - ris nó - bis.
(Do not be angry with us forever.)

103

Kyrie Eleison

MASS XVIII

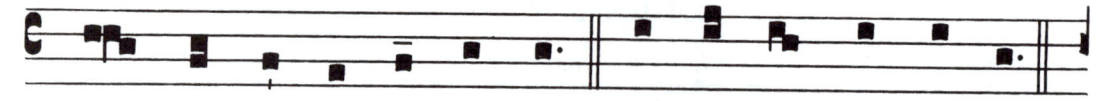

Ký - ri - e e - lé - i - son. *iij.* Chrí - ste e - lé - i - son. *iij.*
(Lord, have mercy on us.) (Christ, have mercy on us.)

Ký - ri - e e - lé - i - son. *ij.* Ký - ri - e e - lé - i - son.

This group of three notes ♪ contains a *quilisma*. It is the little jagged note in the middle. The note before the *quilisma* should be held a little longer and the *quilisma* should be sung very softly.

A man beloved of God and men, whose memory is in benediction.

Joseph, Our Protector

1. Jo - seph, our pro - tec - tor, dwell with - in this house,
   Pa - tron of our fam - 'ly, Ma - ry's Ho - ly spouse.
2. Je - sus, our dear Broth - er, Lord of sky and sea,
   Love and true sub - jec - tion ev - er paid to Thee.

Saint Joseph's Song

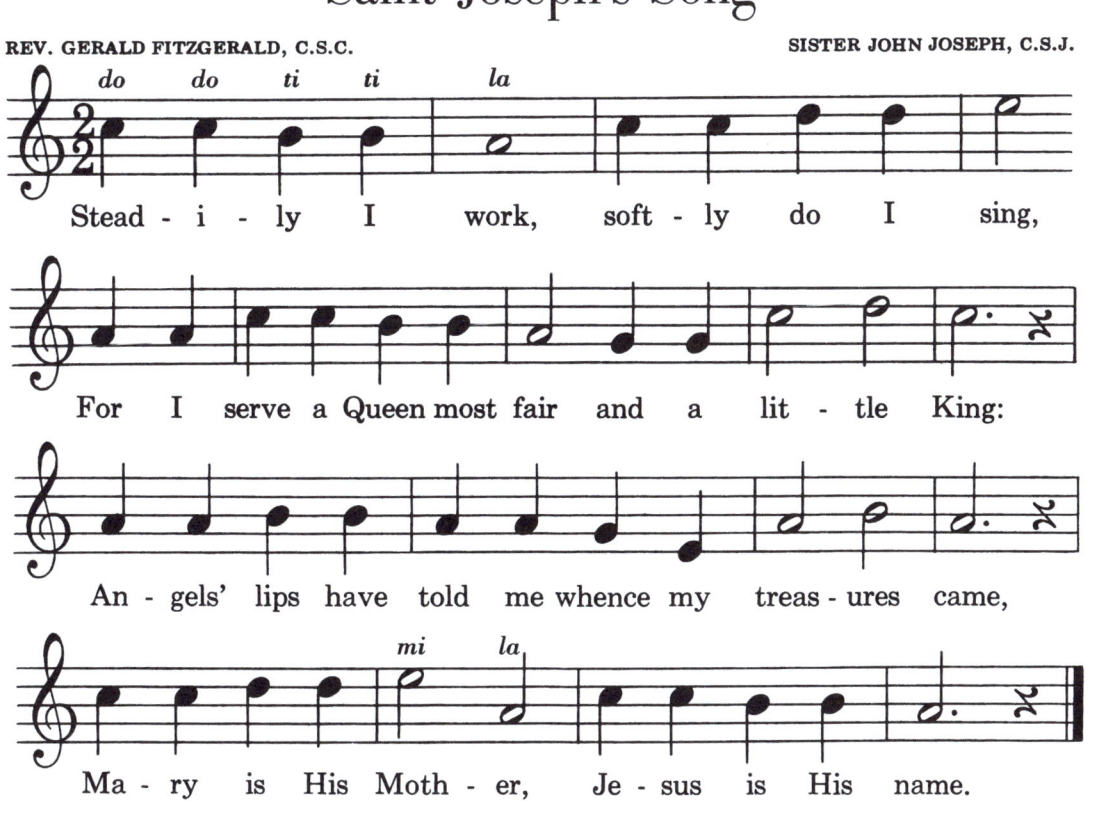

REV. GERALD FITZGERALD, C.S.C. SISTER JOHN JOSEPH, C.S.J.

do do ti ti la

Stead - i - ly I work, soft - ly do I sing,

For I serve a Queen most fair and a lit - tle King:

An - gels' lips have told me whence my treas - ures came,

mi la

Ma - ry is His Moth - er, Je - sus is His name.

I Am the Wind

LOLIA LITTLEHALES

1. I am the wind ver-y strong and bold:
2. I am the wind that you like to know,

I make you shiv-er when the weath-er is cold.
The warm spring wind that makes the daf-fo-dils grow.

We may have snow: hear the wind blow.
Gone is the snow; hear the breeze blow.

Hoo - oo - oo. _____
Hoo - oo - oo. _____

How many beats are there in a measure? How do you know?
Tap the beats lightly while you sing.

There Was a Little Ship

TRANSLATED

DUTCH FOLK SONG

1. There was a lit-tle ship a-sail-ing on the sea.
2. And when the storm-winds blew, they sim-ply let them blow;

The cap-tain was a jol - ly man who liked a cup of tea,
They kept the mu - sic go - ing while they wait - ed snug be - low.

And all the sail - ors danced and sang, as hap - py as could be.
The cap-tain drank a cup of tea, the sail - ors sang, "Yo ho."

I'm Glad

CARLA MARIA BIANCHI
ALSATIAN FOLK TUNE

so   fa   re

1. I'm glad the sun is shin - ing. I'm glad the sky is blue.
2. I'm glad the spring is com - ing. I'm glad the win - ter's past.

so do la fa mi so re mi do

I'm glad the fun - ny puss - y wil - lows grow the way they do,
I'm glad the rob - ins and the wrens are fly - ing north at last,

Tra la la la, grow the way they do.
Tra la la la, fly - ing north at last,

Echo

Tra la la la,' grow the way they do.
Tra la la la, fly - ing north at last.

Look at the time signature. How many beats will you count in each measure?

107

I'm the Doctor Eisenbart[1]

Paraphrased from the GERMAN
GERMAN FOLK SONG

1. I'm the Doc-tor Ei-sen-bart, Vil-le-vil-le-vick bom bom,
2. I'm a doc-tor with an art, Vil-le-vil-le-vick bom bom,
(wood sticks) *(drums)*

Peo-ple know I do my part, Vil-le-vil-le-vick bom bom.
Peo-ple think I'm ver-y smart, Vil-le-vil-le-vick bom bom.
(wood sticks) *(drums)*

I make the pa-tients well a-gain, Vil-le-vil-le-vick bom bom bom bom,
I give them pills to ease their pain, Vil-le-vil-le-vick bom bom bom bom,
(wood sticks) *(drums)*

The ill are nev-er ill a-gain, Vil-le-vil-le-vick bom bom.
They nev-er have to come a-gain, Vil-le-vil-le-vick bom bom.
(wood sticks) *(drums)*

[1] Pronounce *Eye-zen-bahrt*.

The Busy Tailors

DAVID KENTON GERMAN FOLK TUNE

so do

1. Oh, far a-way there's a fun-ny town where tai-lors meet ev-'ry day.
2. These bus-y tai-lors who meet each day tell tales a-gain and a-gain.

There are nine-ty-nine and nine-ty more who come from nine-ty miles or more,
They can tell them nine and nine-ty times, some nine and nine-ty times or more,

Some nine-ty miles or more.
Some nine-ty times or more.

ti re so   so ti re

Nick-y, nick-y, nick, the tai-lor men, nick-y, nick-y, nick, they're cut-ting.
Zip-py, zip-py, zip, the tai-lor men, zip-py, zip-py, zip, they're sew-ing.

Nick-y, nick-y, nick, the tai-lor men, nick-y, nick-y, nick, they're cut-ting.
Zip-py, zip-py, zip, the tai-lor men, zip-py, zip-py, zip, they're sew-ing.

Seven Frogs

Translated by CHRISTINE TURNER CURTIS

DUTCH FOLK SONG
Arranged

1. Sev - en frogs were drows - ing with - in a shal - low pool;
2. Soon the gen - tle spring-time came danc - ing down the hill.

They were near - ly froz - en, the day was ver - y cool.
All the frogs and peep - ers be - gan to pipe and trill,

Up spoke Fa - ther Frog, "Spring is com - ing soon.
Croak - ing long and loud from the pools and bogs.

Can't you hear the night - in - gale re - hearse his fool - ish tune?"
I pre - fer a night - in - gale to half a mil - lion frogs.

How many phrases are alike in this song?
Notice that in the second measure the second note is held longest.
Sing the melody with music syllables before you sing the words.

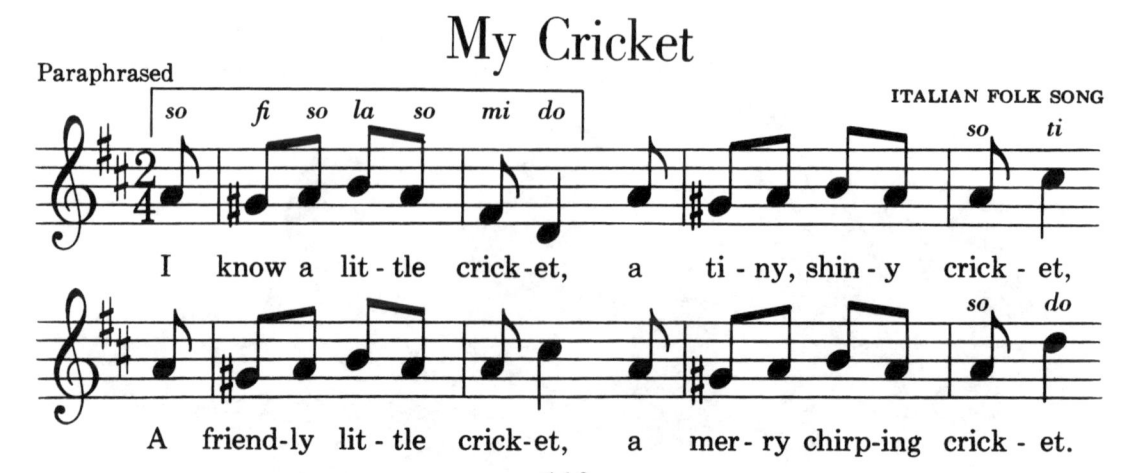

My Cricket

Paraphrased

ITALIAN FOLK SONG

I know a lit - tle crick - et, a ti - ny, shin - y crick - et,

A friend - ly lit - tle crick - et, a mer - ry chirp - ing crick - et.

He lives be-neath my win-dow, right un-der-neath my win-dow,

so fi so la ti do

He's chirp-ing at my win-dow, and sing-ing me to sleep.

When there is a sharp before *fa* it changes its name to *fi* and it sounds a little higher than *fa*.

Robin Hood and Little John

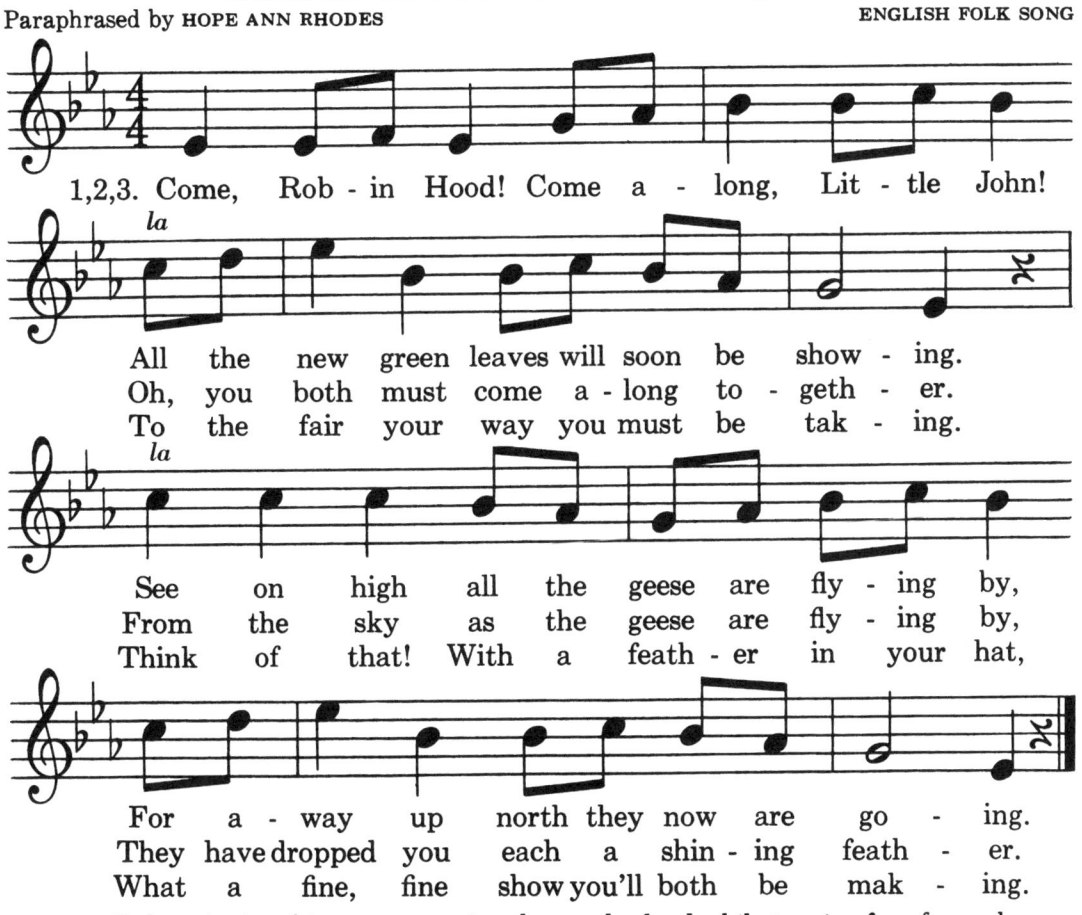

Paraphrased by HOPE ANN RHODES

ENGLISH FOLK SONG

1,2,3. Come, Rob-in Hood! Come a-long, Lit-tle John!

All the new green leaves will soon be show-ing.
Oh, you both must come a-long to-geth-er.
To the fair your way you must be tak-ing.

See on high all the geese are fly-ing by,
From the sky as the geese are fly-ing by,
Think of that! With a feath-er in your hat,

For a-way up north they now are go-ing.
They have dropped you each a shin-ing feath-er.
What a fine, fine show you'll both be mak-ing.

Before singing this song try saying the words aloud while tapping four for each measure. You may be able to sing all the syllables without the help of your teacher.

Three flats tell you that *do* is on the first line.

OUR LADY

Our Lady helped her mother
To wash the breakfast things,
And in the garden Gabriel
Waited with folded wings.

Our Lady came to the garden
For lettuce and for peas,
And Gabriel knelt to worship her,
Humbly, on his knees.

Our Lady's soul was shining,
The light was in her face—
"Hail full of grace," said Gabriel,
"Hail, Mary, full of grace."

Marigold Hunt

The Annunciation

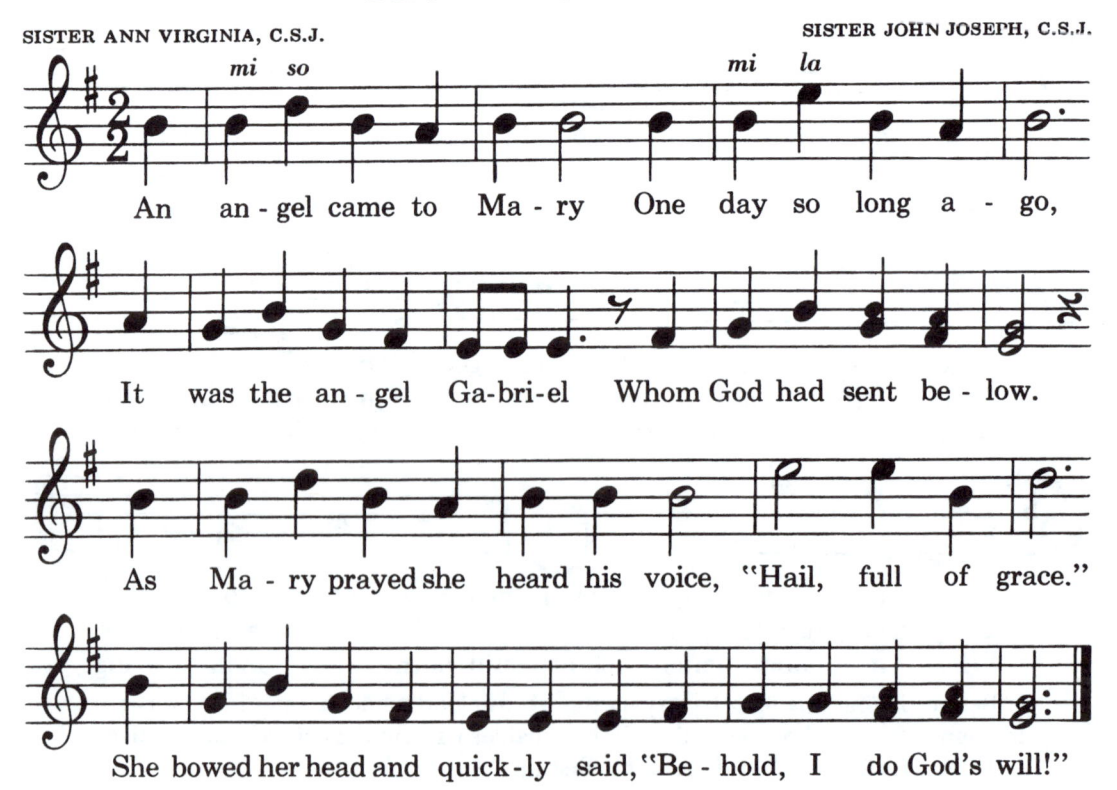

SISTER ANN VIRGINIA, C.S.J.   SISTER JOHN JOSEPH, C.S.J.

An an-gel came to Ma-ry One day so long a-go,
It was the an-gel Ga-bri-el Whom God had sent be-low.
As Ma-ry prayed she heard his voice, "Hail, full of grace."
She bowed her head and quick-ly said, "Be-hold, I do God's will!"

Mother of Christ

JAN BEZDEK

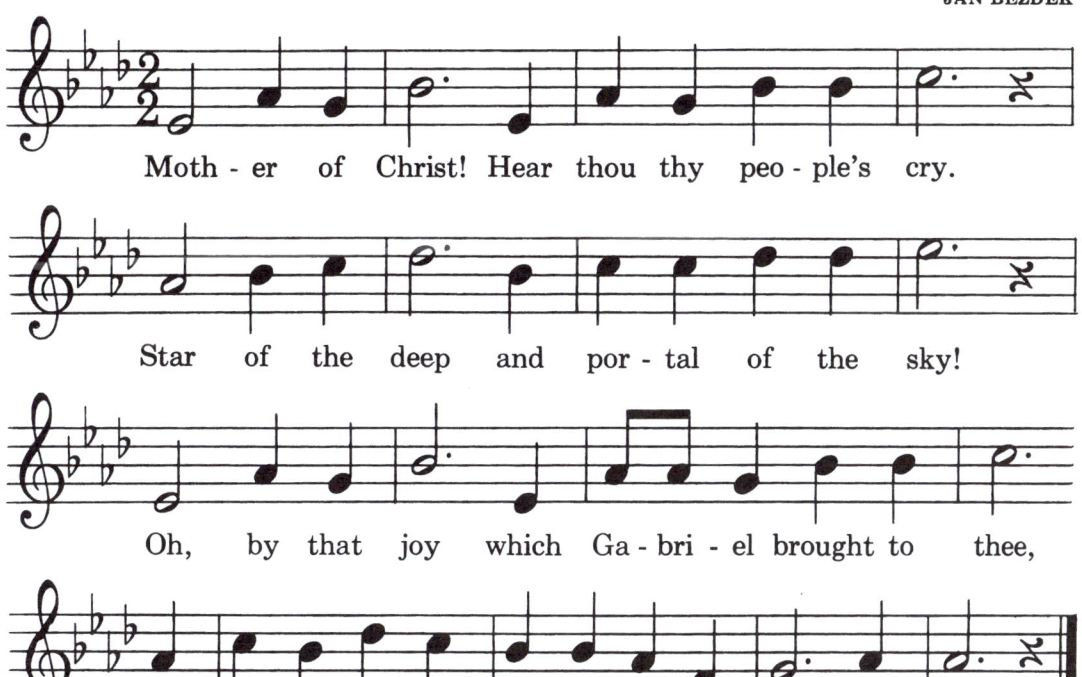

Moth - er of Christ! Hear thou thy peo - ple's cry.

Star of the deep and por - tal of the sky!

Oh, by that joy which Ga - bri - el brought to thee,

Thou Vir - gin first and last, Let us thy Mer - cy see.

Forgive Us Our Sins, O Lord

For - give us our sins, O Lord: help us, O God, our Sav - ior.

And for the hon - or of Thy Name, O Lord, de - liv - er us.

The River

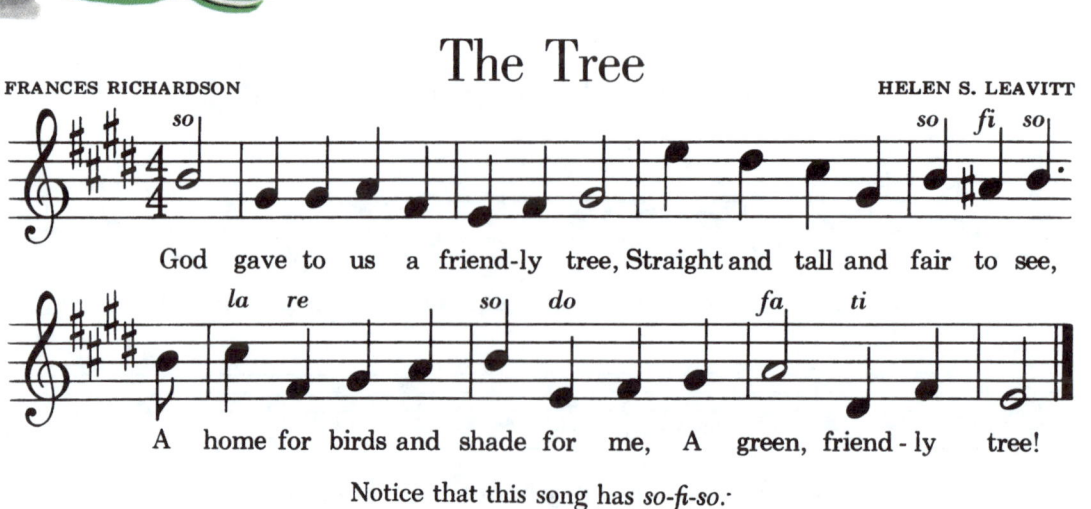

OLD IRISH SONG

1. Pray tell me how deep is yonder river?
2. Pray tell me how I can cross that river?

Tra la la la la la, tra la la la la la.
Tra la la la la la, tra la la la la la.

A stone thrown in will find the bottom.
The ducks and geese, they swim it over.

Tra la la la la la la.
Tra la la la la la la.

The Tree

FRANCES RICHARDSON
HELEN S. LEAVITT

God gave to us a friend-ly tree, Straight and tall and fair to see,
A home for birds and shade for me, A green, friend-ly tree!

Notice that this song has *so-fi-so.*

Down in the Valley

KENTUCKY MOUNTAIN FOLK SONG

1. Down in the valley, the valley so low,
Hang your head over, hear the wind blow,
Hear the wind blow, dear, oh, hear the wind blow,
Hang your head over, hear the wind blow.

2. Roses love sunshine and vi-'lets love dew,
Angels in heaven know I love you.
Know I love you, dear, they know I love you,
Angels in heaven know I love you.

Old Folks at Home

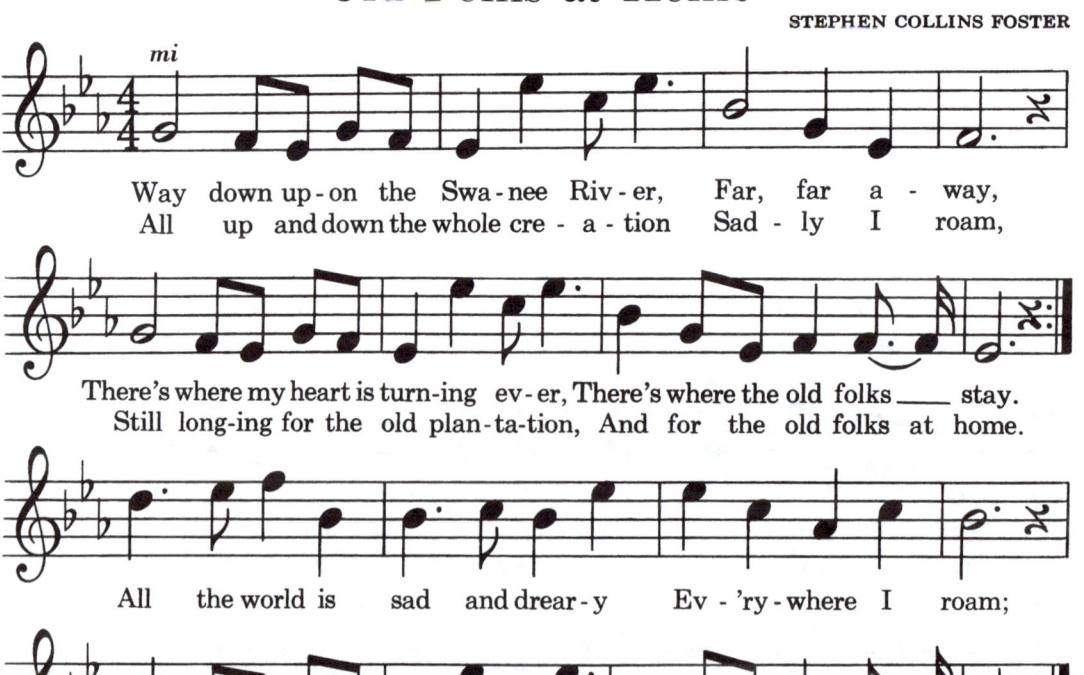

STEPHEN COLLINS FOSTER

Way down up-on the Swa-nee Riv-er, Far, far a-way,
All up and down the whole cre-a-tion Sad-ly I roam,

There's where my heart is turn-ing ev-er, There's where the old folks ___ stay.
Still long-ing for the old plan-ta-tion, And for the old folks at home.

All the world is sad and drear-y Ev-'ry-where I roam;

O loved ones, how my heart grows wea-ry, Far from the old folks at home.

Ring, Ring the Banjo!

STEPHEN COLLINS FOSTER

1. The time is nev-er drear-y If a fel-low nev-er groans;
2. Oh! nev-er count the bub-bles While there's wa-ter in the spring.

The la-dies nev-er wea-ry With the rat-tle of the bones.
A fel-low has no trou-bles While he's got this song to sing.

Then come a-gain, Su-san-na, By the gas-light of the moon;
The beau-ties of cre-a-tion Will nev-er lose their charm

We'll turn the old pi-an-o When the ban-jo's out of tune.
While I roam the old plan-ta-tion With my true love on my arm.

CHORUS

Ring, ring the ban-jo! I like that good old song.

Come a-gain my true love; Oh, where you been so long?

117

'Liza Jane

TRADITIONAL

1. There's a girl in Bal-ti-more, Li'l 'Li-za Jane,
2. If you'll come and be my own, Li'l 'Li-za Jane,
3. We'll have chick-ens round our door, Li'l 'Li-za Jane,

She's the one that I a-dore, Li'l 'Li-za Jane.
We'll eat ham and sweet corn pone, Li'l 'Li-za Jane.
Brus-sels car-pet on our floor, Li'l 'Li-za Jane.

Chorus

O E-li-za, li'l 'Li-za Jane, O E-li-za, li'l 'Li-za Jane.

The Pawpaw Patch

AMERICAN SINGING GAME

1. Where,___ oh where is dear___ lit-tle Ma-ry?
2. Come___ on, boys, and let's___ go___ find her,
3. Scoop-ing up paw-paws, put them in a bas-ket,

Where,___ oh where is dear___ lit-tle Ma-ry?
Come___ on, boys, and let's___ go___ find her,
Scoop-ing up paw-paws, put them in a bas-ket,

Where,___ oh where is dear___ lit-tle Ma-ry?
Come___ on, boys, and let's___ go___ find her,
Scoop-ing up paw-paws, put them in a bas-ket,

1,2,3. 'Way down yon-der in the paw-paw patch.

Form two lines of several couples, partners facing.

Stanza 1. As the group sings, "Where, oh, where is dear little Mary" (or sing the name of the girl at the head of her line), the girl in the first couple turns right and skips down behind the line of girls, and then around behind the line of boys and back to her place.

Stanza 2. The same girl continues to skip around the group, but this time she beckons the boys to follow her. They do so, one behind the other, until all are back in place.

STANZA 3. Partners join hands and follow the first couple in the same direction that *Mary* skipped in the beginning. When the first couple reaches the foot of the group they form an arch, under which the other couples skip to their places. Each time the word "scooping" is sung, the players pretend they are bending over to scoop up pawpaws. The second couple now becomes the first, and the game continues until each girl has had her turn at being *Mary*.

Easter

This is the day which the Lord has made;
let us be glad and rejoice in it.
Gradual—Easter Sunday

Alleluia

Al - le - lú - ia, al - le - lú - ia, al - le - lú - ia.

Gló - ri - a Pa - tri et Fí - li - o* et Spi - rí - tu - i Sán - cto.
(Repeat Alleluia.)

Sing the small note in the third Alleluia softly.
Where do you find *do* in this chant?
How many times can you find a *podatus* (▪)?

O Filii et Filiae

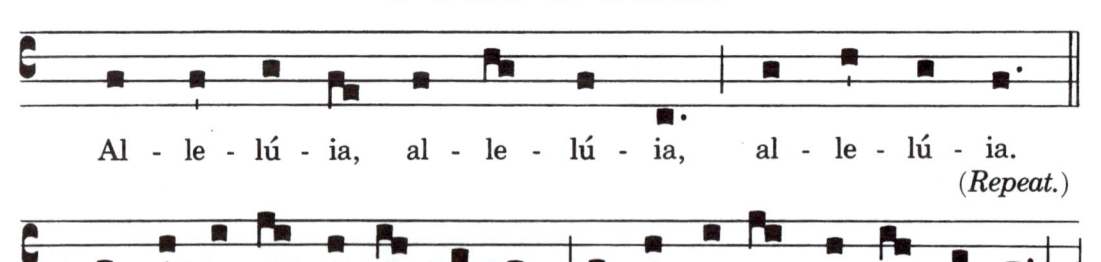

Al - le - lú - ia, al - le - lú - ia, al - le - lú - ia.
(Repeat.)

O fí - li - i et fí - li - ae, Rex cae - lés - tis, Rex glo - ri - ae,
Ye sons and daugh-ters of the Lord, The King of glo - ry, King a - dored,

Mór - te sur - ré - xit hó - di - e, Al - le - lú - ia. ℟ Alleluia.
This day Him-self from death re - stored, Al - le - lu - ia. ℟ Alleluia.

Count the number of times you find a *clivis* (▪) in this chant.
The *do* clef will tell you where to find *do*.

Hymn of Praise

GIOVANNI PALESTRINA

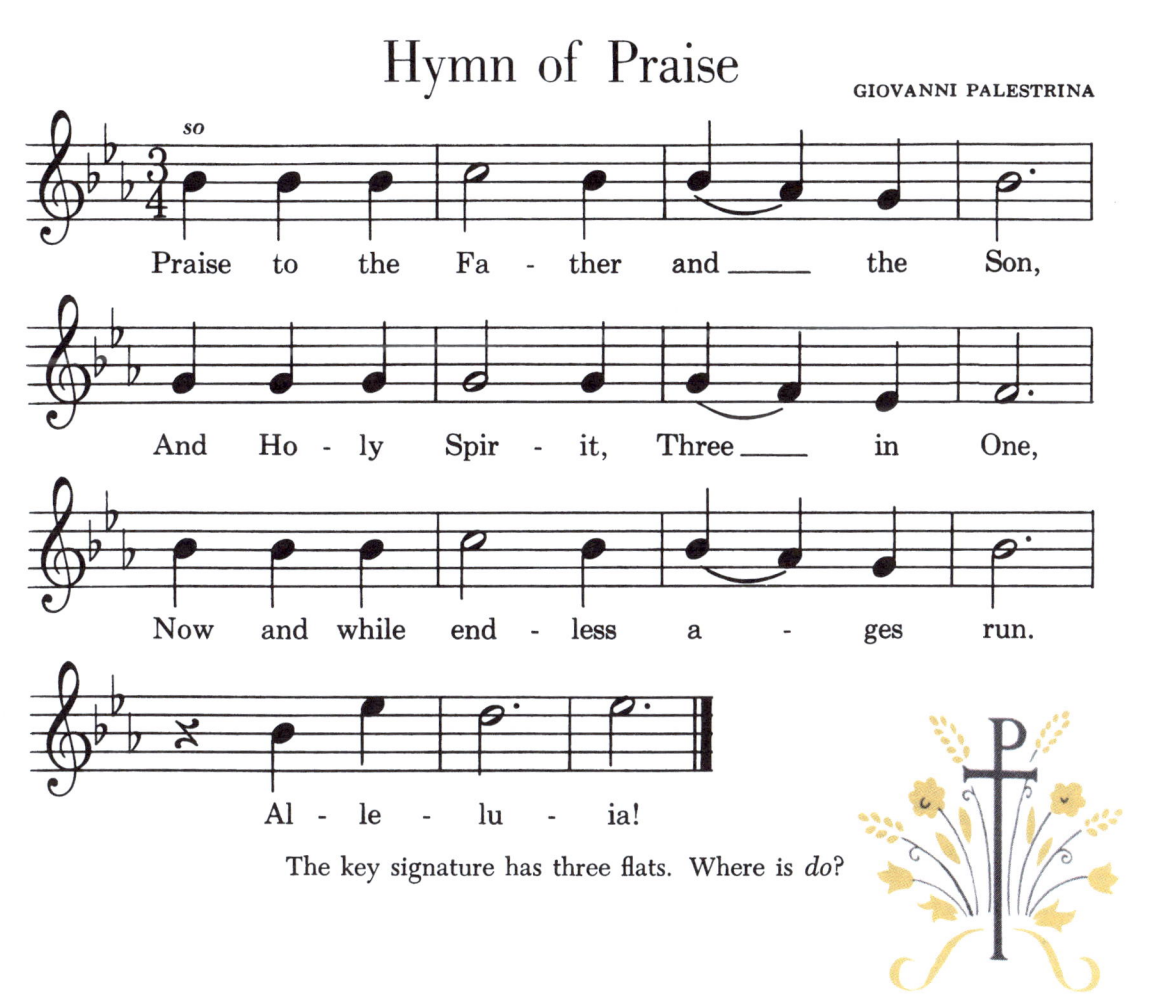

Praise to the Father and the Son,
And Holy Spirit, Three in One,
Now and while endless ages run.
Al-le-lu-ia!

The key signature has three flats. Where is *do*?

At Easter Time

LAURA RICHARDS
SISTER JOHN JOSEPH, C.S.J.

1. The lit-tle flow'rs came through the ground, At East-er time, at East-er time;
They raised their heads and looked a-round, At hap-py East-er time.
2. And ev-'ry pret-ty bud did say, "Good peo-ple, bless this ho-ly day,
For Christ is ris'n, the an-gels say, At hap-py East-er time!"

Three Little Chickens

UNKNOWN   SALLY ANDERSON

Said the first little chick-en, with a queer little squirm,

"Oh, I wish I could find a fat little worm!"

Said the next little chick-en, with an odd little shrug,

"Oh, I wish I could find a fat little bug!"

Said the third little chick-en, with a sharp little squeal,

"Oh, I wish I could find some nice yel-low meal!"

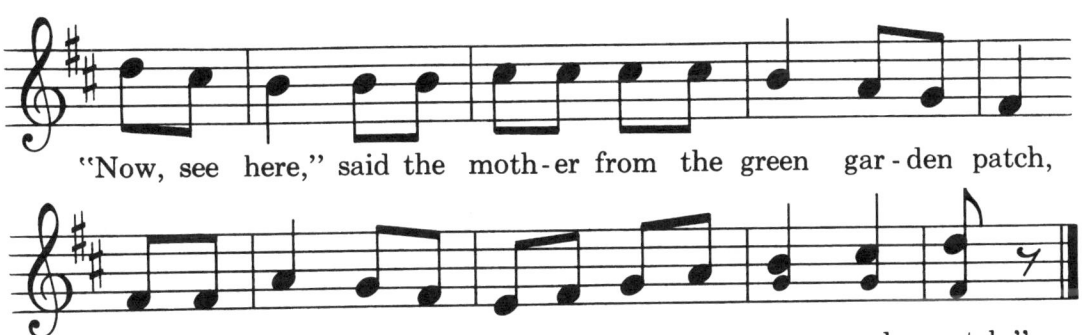

"Now, see here," said the moth-er from the green gar-den patch,

"If you want an-y break-fast you must come and scratch."

Greedy Ducks

ETHEL CROWNINSHIELD
GERMAN FOLK TUNE

so   mi

1. A moth-er and her duck-lings Came swim-ming to the shore;
2. Those greed-y lit-tle duck-lings, Like man-y folks I've met,

I gave those ducks my pop-corn, But still they cried for more.
Are al-ways want-ing more things No mat-ter what they get.

so   so   so

Quack, quack, quack, quack, quack, quack, quack, quack! But still they cried for more!
Quack, quack, quack, quack, quack, quack, quack, quack! No mat-ter what they get!

Quack, quack, quack, quack, quack, quack, quack, quack! But still they cried for more!
Quack, quack, quack, quack, quack, quack, quack, quack! No mat-ter what they get!

Notice the time signature.
How many times will you tap in a measure?
How many eighth notes do you sing to one tap?

The Land of the Dutch, Dutch, Dutch

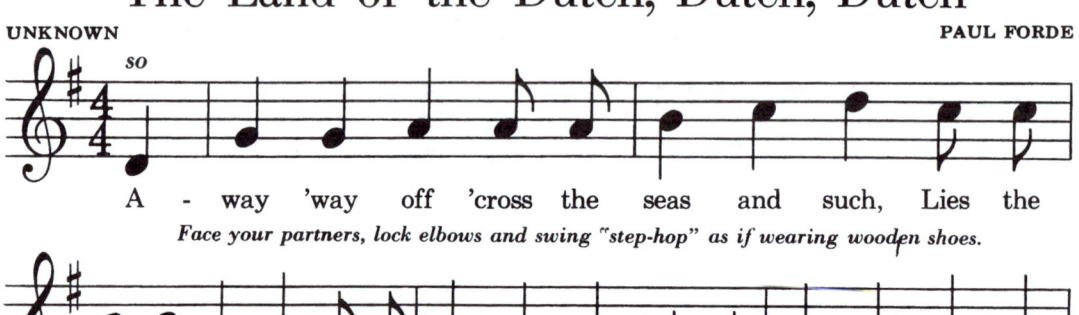

UNKNOWN PAUL FORDE

A - way 'way off 'cross the seas and such, Lies the
Face your partners, lock elbows and swing "step-hop" as if wearing wooden shoes.

lit - tle flat land of the Dutch, Dutch, Dutch! Where the wind-mills' arms go
Partners face with outstretched arms, imitate windmills.

round, round, round, And sing to the cows with a creak - y sound, Where
Imitate

storks live up in the chim - ney top, And wood - en shoes pound
stork standing on one foot. *Stand still.*

plop, plop, plop! Where milk cans shine in the shin - i - est way, And the
Stamp. *Boys shine milk cans.*

house maids scrub, scrub, scrub all day. Oh, that lit-tle toy land, I
Girls scrub.   *Dance as at beginning.*

like it much, That prim lit-tle, trim lit-tle land of the Dutch.
                                                                      Stamp, stamp, stamp.

Do you know that every phrase has the same melody? How many phrases are there?

Spring Music

SHEILA GALVIN   DANISH

The bum-ble-bee is hum-ming, The rob-in's here a-gain,

He sings of sun-ny morn-ings And splash-ing A-pril rain,

A hur-dy-gur-dy's play-ing A-long the cit-y street,

Its mu-sic sets the rhy-thm For chil-dren's danc-ing feet.

Can you find any difference between the second and fourth phrases?

125

Four in a Boat

SINGING GAME

1. Four in a boat and the tide rolls high,
2. Get me a pretty one, stay all day,
3. Eight in a boat and it won't go round,

Four in a boat and the tide rolls high,
Get me a pretty one, stay all day,
Eight in a boat and it won't go round,

Get you a pretty one bye and bye,
We don't care what the others say,
Swing that pretty one you've just found,

Get you a pretty one bye and bye.
We don't care what the others say.
Swing that pretty one you've just found.

Form a single circle, hands joined, facing center. Four boys in center (inner circle), hands joined, facing outer circle. *Stanza 1.* Outer circle skips or walks around to the left. Inner circle does the same in the opposite direction. *Stanza 2.* All drop hands and both circles move in the same direction. Each boy in center chooses a girl in the outer circle and walks beside her until the end of the stanza.

Stanza 3. Each boy in the center pulls his partner into the inner circle. Both circles join hands and move in opposite directions, as in the first stanza. They pretend that the boat won't go around until "Swing that pretty one," when each boy in the inner circle swings his partner, hands joined, and then leaves her in the center. The song is repeated with girls in the center.

Have You Ever Seen the Daisies?

SISTER JOHN JOSEPH, C.S.J.

Not too fast

Have you ev-er seen the dai-sies bloom-ing In the sun-light, in the spring?

Have you ev-er seen the wa-ter spar-kling In the sun-light, in the spring?

Have you ev-er seen the white clouds Sail-ing soft-ly a-gainst the blue?

Have you ev-er thought that all this beau-ty God has made for me and you?

The Mother Moon

UNKNOWN　　　　　　　　　　　　　　　　　　　　ENGLISH FOLK TUNE

1. The moth-er moon is float-ing high, She's filled with sil-ver light,
2. And just be-fore the morn-ing comes, To col-or clouds with red,
3. She cov-ers them with fleec-y clouds, Then tip-toes through the sky,

do ti la si la ti si la

To make the mead-ows of the sky So love-ly and so bright.
She gath-ers up the lit-tle stars And tucks them in-to bed.
And sings un-til they fall a-sleep A star-ry lull-a-by.

Notice that two notes near the end of the song are called *si*.

127

All the Birds Will Soon Be Here

TRANSLATED
GERMAN FOLK SONG

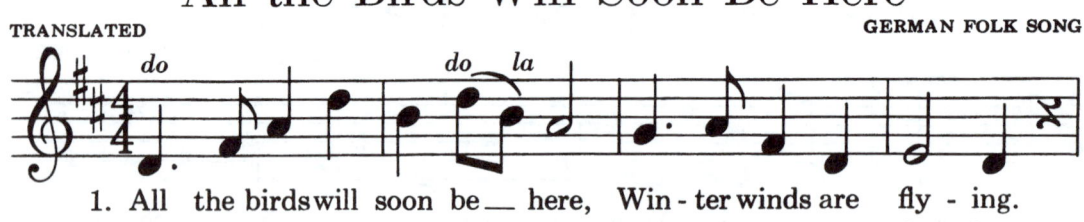

1. All the birds will soon be here, Win-ter winds are fly-ing.
2. Mer-ry birds are on the wing, North-ward they are fly-ing.

Love-ly mu-sic soon will sound, Chirp-ing, pip-ing, all a-round,
Rob-in, star-ling, thrush and swal-low, Scold-ing blue jay, sing-ing spar-row,

Twit-ter-ing and coo-ing too. Spring will soon be com-ing.
Bob-o-link and blue-bird too. Spring will soon be com-ing.

The Bumblebee

TRADITIONAL
SISTER ROSE MARGARET, C.S.J.

Gaily

1. The bum-ble-bee, the bum-ble-bee,
2. The bum-ble-bee, the bum-ble-bee,

He flew to the top of the tu-lip tree:
He flew far a-way from the tu-lip tree:

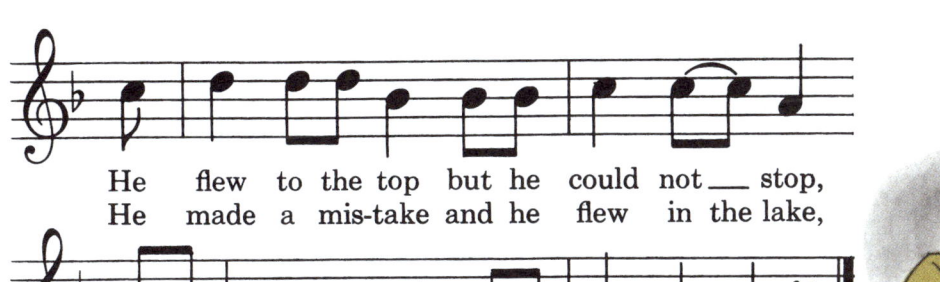

He flew to the top but he could not stop,
He made a mis-take and he flew in the lake,

For he had to get home to his ear-ly tea.
And he nev-er got home to his ear-ly tea.

Do is in the first space. What is the syllable name of the first note?

The Brown Bird

**After the original
by CHRISTINE TURNER CURTIS**

PUERTO RICAN FOLK SONG

1. There's a ti-ny brown bird on the ga-ble sing-ing, ___
2. May the skies bless her slum-ber while she is rest-ing, ___

Lull-a-by and sweet dreams to my dear one bring-ing. ___
And the ti-ny brown bird in the leaves is nest-ing. ___

Sing, mer-ry song-bird, where she is sleep-ing, ___
Sing, drow-sy song-bird, care-less of sor-row, ___

And the an-gels a-bove her their watch are keep-ing. ___
May she dream on in safe-ty un-til to-mor-row. ___

There is one sharp at the beginning of the song. This key signature tells you that *do* is on the second line.

129

Old Man Thunder

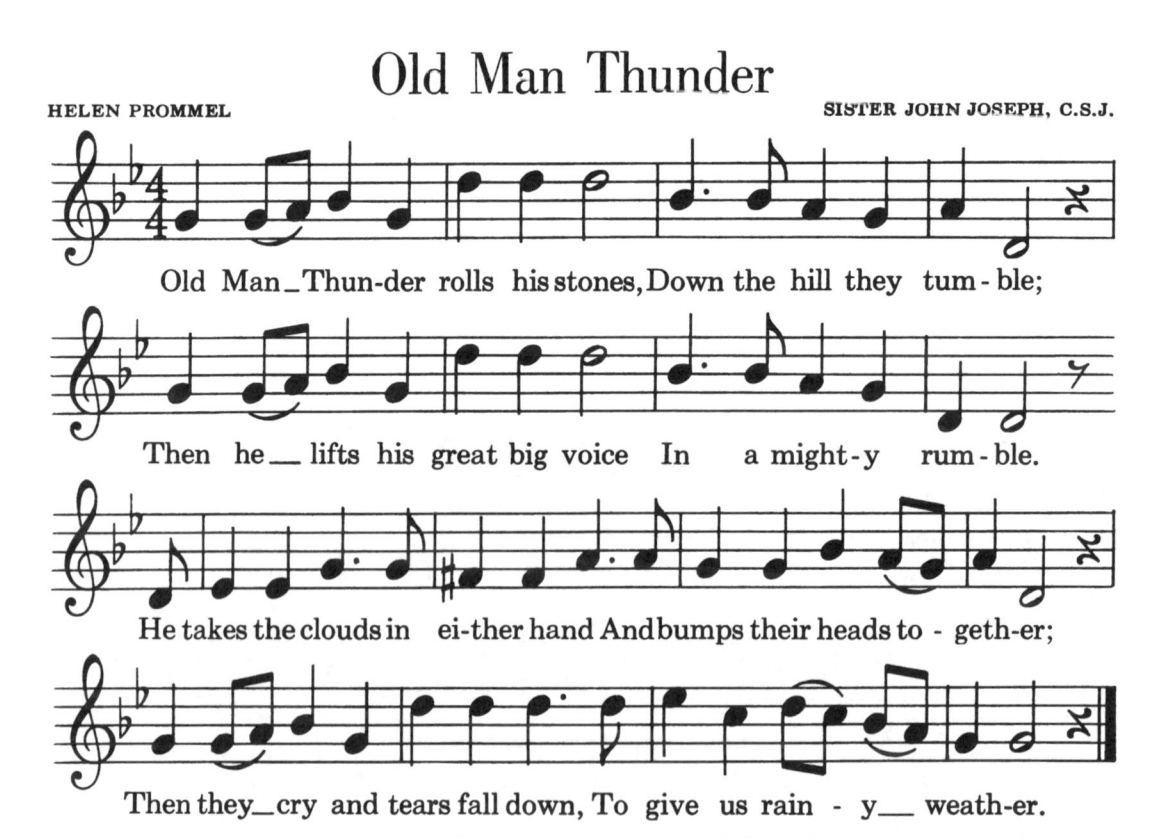

HELEN PROMMEL
SISTER JOHN JOSEPH, C.S.J.

Old Man Thun-der rolls his stones, Down the hill they tum-ble;
Then he lifts his great big voice In a might-y rum-ble.
He takes the clouds in ei-ther hand And bumps their heads to-geth-er;
Then they cry and tears fall down, To give us rain-y weath-er.

Do you remember how to sing the dotted quarter note followed by an eighth note?

My heart leaps up when I behold
A rainbow in the sky. . . .

The Rainbow

ELLEN MURRAY
WOLFGANG AMADEUS MOZART

1. There's a rain-bow in the sky like a bridge of gold and blue,
2. When the storm clouds roll a-way and the sky is clean and bright,

Like an arch of rose and pearl that the sun is shin-ing through.
Then the love-ly rain-bow glows like a path of col-ored light.

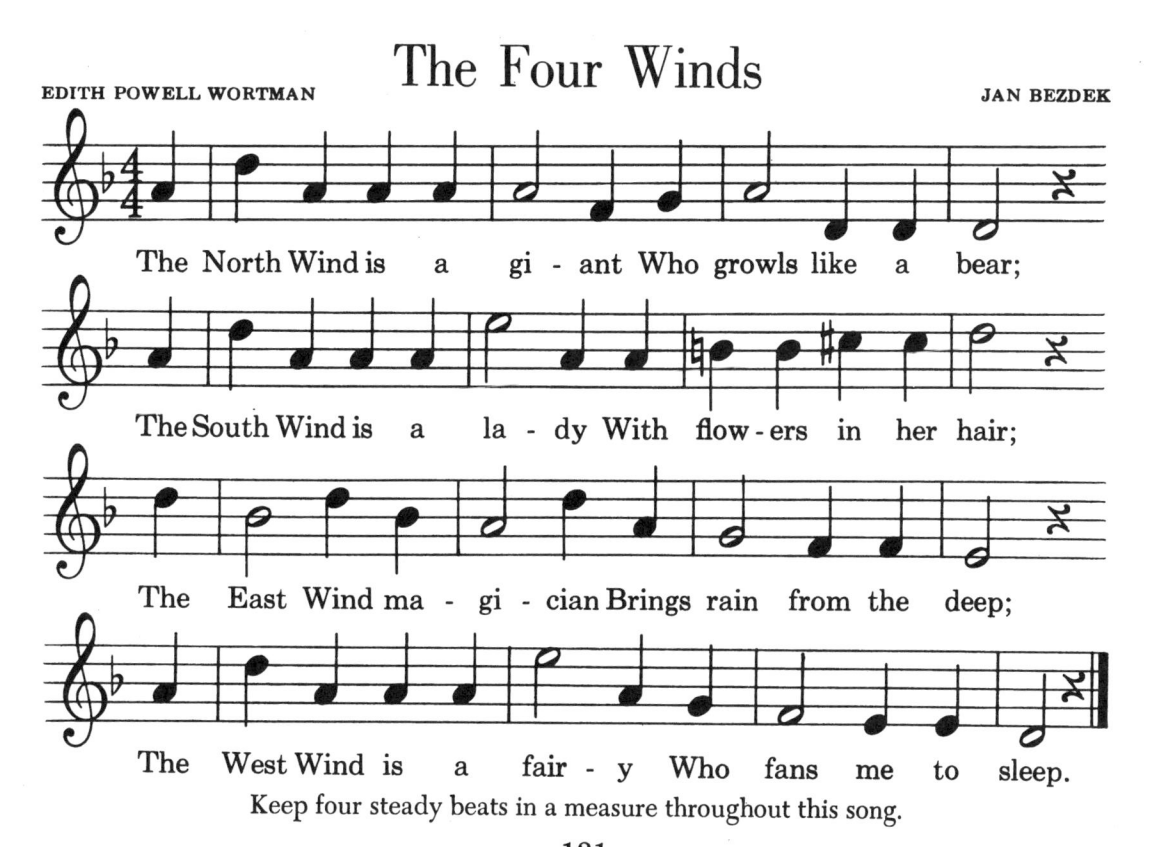

The Four Winds

EDITH POWELL WORTMAN
JAN BEZDEK

The North Wind is a gi - ant Who growls like a bear;

The South Wind is a la - dy With flow-ers in her hair;

The East Wind ma - gi - cian Brings rain from the deep;

The West Wind is a fair - y Who fans me to sleep.

Keep four steady beats in a measure throughout this song.

131

Little Brown Brother

E. NESBIT
MARK NOLAN

1. Lit - tle brown broth-er, oh, lit - tle brown broth-er,
Are you a - wake in the dark?
Here we lie co - si - ly, close to each oth - er:
Hark to the song of the lark!

2. "Wak - en," the lark says, "a - wak - en and dress you,
Put on your green coats and gay,
Sun - light will smile on you, rain will ca - ress you,
Wak - en! 'tis morn - ing, 'tis May!"

Indian Lullaby

MOISELLE RENSTROM

la ti do la si la ti si la mi re do ti do la

1. In a moss - y lin - den cra - dle, Hung be-neath the sway-ing trees,
Sleeps the lit - tle In - dian ba - by, Gen - tly rocked by ev - 'ry breeze.

2. In - dian ba - by, you are wak - ing; Big black eyes you o - pen wide.
At your moth - er you are smil - ing, As she's stand - ing by your side.

la   la   so   so

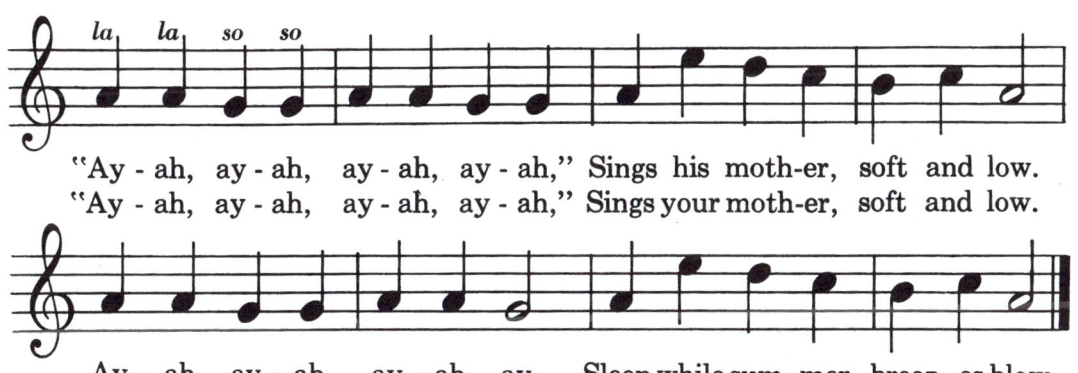

"Ay - ah, ay - ah, ay - ah, ay - ah," Sings his moth-er, soft and low.
"Ay - ah, ay - ah, ay - ah, ay - ah," Sings your moth-er, soft and low.

Ay - ah, ay - ah, ay - ah, ay. Sleep while sum-mer breez-es blow.
Ay - ah, ay - ah, ay - ah, ay. Sleep while sum-mer breez-es blow.

How many times do you hear the tune of the third and fourth measures?

Jesus, Tender Shepherd, Hear Me

S. R. M.

1. Je - sus, ten - der Shep - herd,___ hear me.
2. All the day Thy hand has ___ led me

do ti la si la ti do la ti

Bless Thy___ lit - tle___ child to - night,
And I ___ thank Thee___ for Thy care.

Through the dark - ness be Thou___ near me,
Thou hast warmed and clothed and ___ fed me.

Keep me___ safe till___ morn - ing light.
Lis - ten___ to my___ eve - ning pray'r.

If the song ended with the second phrase would it sound like a completed song?

133

Home on the Range

COWBOY SONG

1. Oh, give me a home where the buf - fa - lo roam,
2. How of - ten at night, when the heav - ens are bright

Where the deer and the an - te - lope play,
With the light from the glit - ter - ing stars,

Where seldom is heard a dis - cour - ag - ing word,
Have I stood there a - mazed and asked as I gazed,

And the skies are not cloud-y all day.
If their glo-ry ex-ceeds that of ours.

Chorus

Home, home on the range __ Where the deer and the an-te-lope play, __

Where sel-dom is heard a dis-cour-ag-ing word,

And the skies are not cloud-y all day.

While the Balalaikas Play

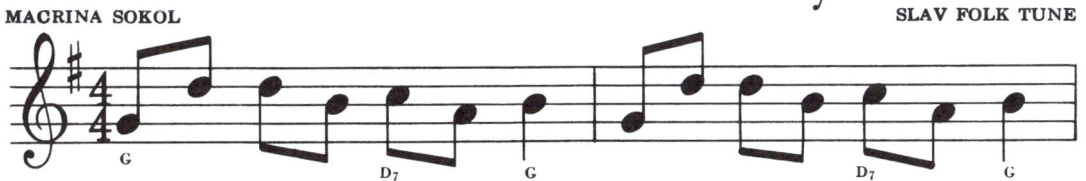

MACRINA SOKOL
SLAV FOLK TUNE

1. Tan-ya, come and dance with me, mu-sic's sound-ing mer-ri-ly,
2. You will be the fair-est there, rib-bons in your shin-ing hair.

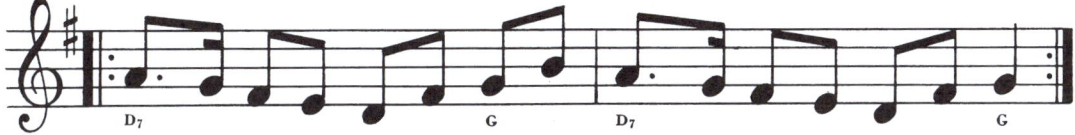

Ev-'ry-bod-y's whirl-ing twirl-ing, while the bal-a-lai-kas play!
Tan-ya, come and join the danc-ing while the bal-a-lai-kas play!

The signs ‖: :‖ tell you that all the music between them is repeated.

135

Up Yonder

Translated by MARGARETA WASSALI

SWISS FOLK SONG

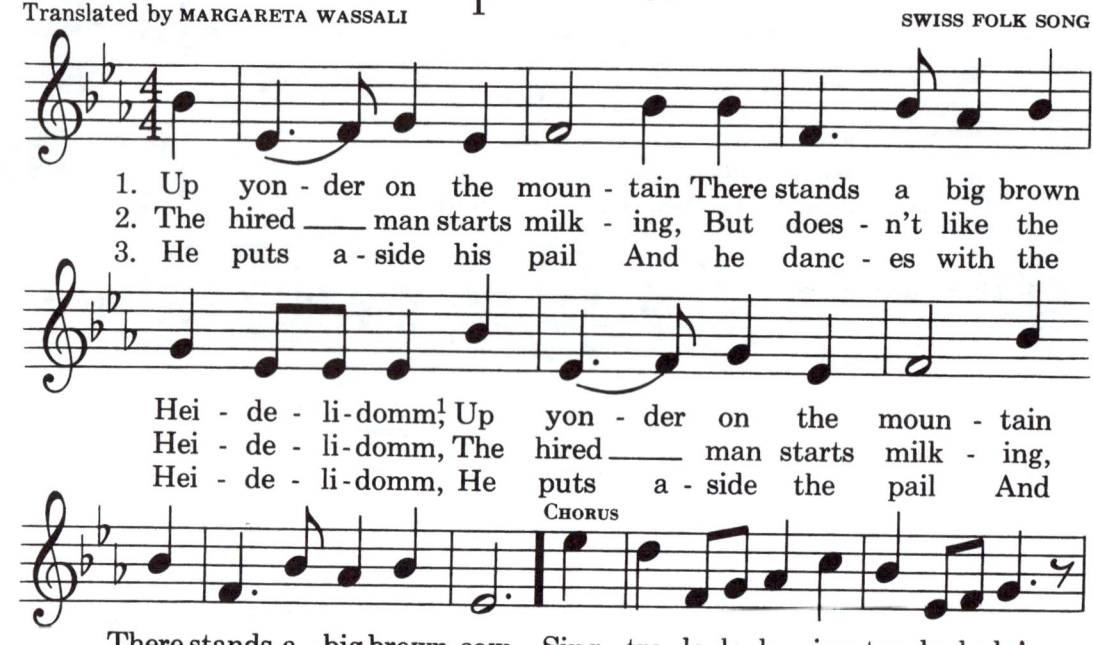

1. Up yonder on the mountain There stands a big brown cow.
2. The hired man starts milking, But doesn't like the job.
3. He puts aside his pail And he dances with the maid.

Heidelidomm,[1] Up yonder on the mountain There stands a big brown cow.
Heidelidomm, The hired man starts milking, But doesn't like the job.
Heidelidomm, He puts aside the pail And he dances with the maid.

Chorus

Sing tra la la la, sing tra la la la! Tra la la la la, sing tra la la! Sing tra la la la, sing tra la la la! Tra la la la la la la la la!

4. And while the two are dancing,
   The cow steps in the Heidelidomm,
   And while the two are dancing,
   The cow steps in the milk.

5. You lazy, lazy milkman,
   Now we have curdled Heidelidomm,
   You lazy, lazy milkman,
   Now we have curdled the milk.

6. The moral of this story,
   Don't try to milk and Heidelidomm,
   The moral of this story,
   Don't try to milk and dance.

[1]Pronounce high-day-lee-dom

Hungarian Dance

After the original by
BLANCHE JENNINGS THOMPSON

HUNGARIAN FOLK SONG

1. Hi hi ya, hi hi ya, hi hi ya, hi!
2. Hi hi ya, hi hi ya, hi hi ya, hi!
3. Hi hi ya, hi hi ya, hi hi ya, hi!

Choose part-ners, choose part-ners, time hur-ries by!
Change part-ners, change part-ners, now off we fly!
Dance fast-er, dance fast-er, rest by and by!

Swing your part-ner round a-bout, hi hi hi!
Swing your part-ner from the floor, hi hi hi!
Whirl-a-whirl-a-whirl a-round, hi hi hi!

Swing your part-ner round a-bout, hi hi hi! *Hi!*
Swing your part-ner from the floor, hi hi hi! *Hi!*
Whirl-a-whirl-a-whirl a-round, hi hi hi! *Hi!*

Form a double circle of couples, girls on the inside facing clockwise, boys on the outside facing counterclockwise. Hands on hips. *Phrase one:* All move in direction they face; starting with left foot, do a "step-hop" polka step. *Phrase two:* Stop and bow (girls curtsy) *to partner. Phrase three:* Link left arms, swing partners, making a complete turn; then face partner and stamp and clap three times on "hi hi hi!" *Phrase four:* Link right arms, swing partners, making a complete turn; then face partners and stamp and clap on "hi hi hi!" On the final "*hi*" (spoken or shouted) kick the heel of right foot on the floor with a forward motion. The dance is repeated through the second and third stanzas, moving gradually faster and faster to the end.

Hickory, Dickory Dock

TRADITIONAL

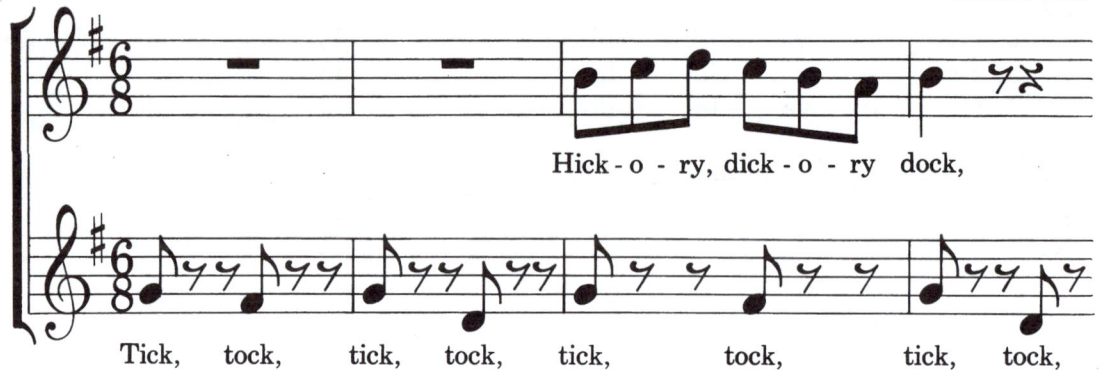

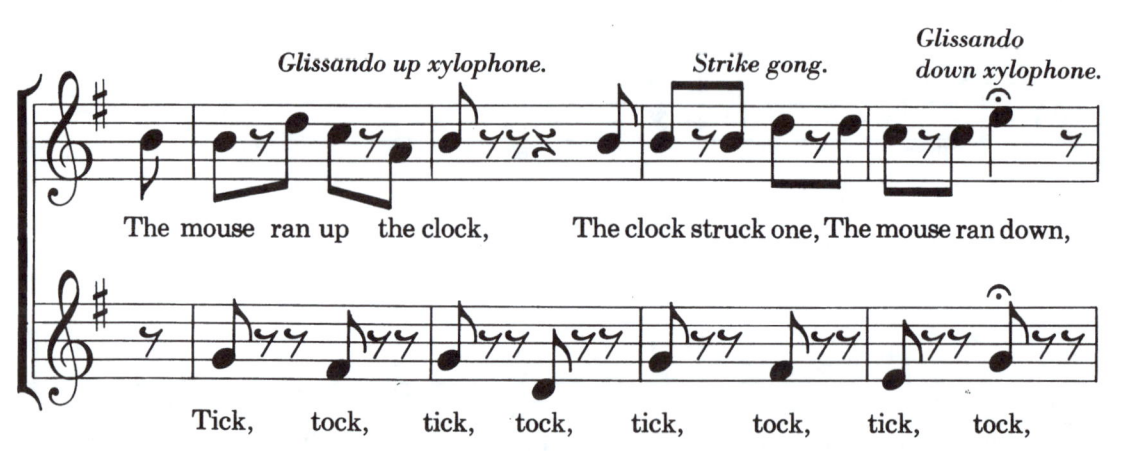

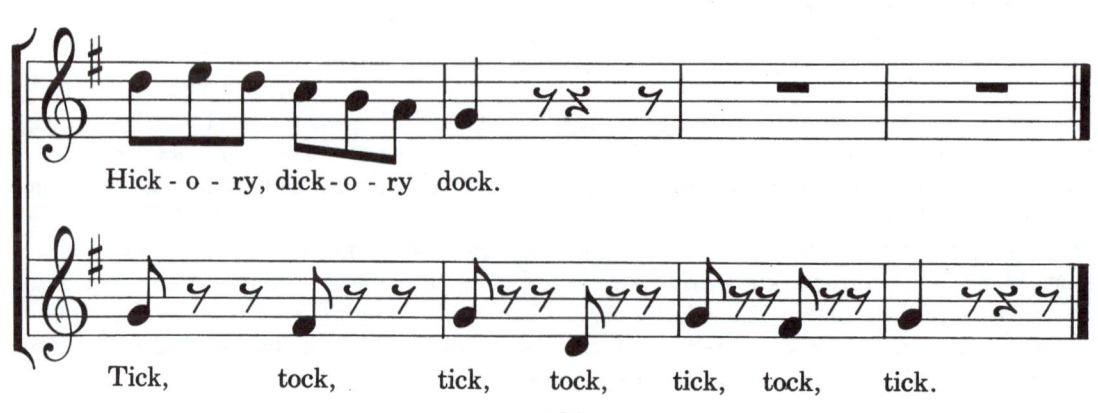

Hick-o-ry, dick-o-ry dock,
Tick, tock, tick, tock, tick, tock, tick, tock,

Glissando up xylophone. *Strike gong.* *Glissando down xylophone.*

The mouse ran up the clock, The clock struck one, The mouse ran down,
Tick, tock, tick, tock, tick, tock, tick, tock,

Hick-o-ry, dick-o-ry dock.
Tick, tock, tick, tock, tick, tock, tick.

The Bell Ringer

FRANCES FORD
FRENCH-CANADIAN FOLK SONG

1. High in the stee - ple hangs the bell,
2. Old Fa - ther Si - mon's gray and worn,

Old Fa - ther Si - mon rings it well.
Old Fa - ther Si - mon's gown is torn.

Ding, dong, ding, ev - 'ry day, ev - 'ry hour,
Ding, dong, ding, if he van - ished a - way,

Ding, dong, ding, sounds the peal from the tow'r.
Ding, dong, ding, we could romp all the day.

Clang, o - ver - head, calls to bed.
Clang, o - ver - head, calls to bed.

Some of you will enjoy singing and playing this bell tune while others sing the song. How many times will you repeat these two measures? What tells you to repeat?

Ding, dong, ding, dong, ding, dong, ding.

Pentecost

The Spirit of the Lord hath filled the whole world. Alleluia, Alleluia.
Introit—Pentecost

Veni Creator Spiritus

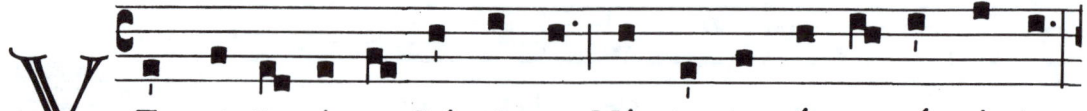

Ve-ni Cre-á-tor Spí-ri-tus, Mén-tes tu-ó-rum ví-si-ta:
(Come, Creator Spirit,) *(Visit the souls of Thy faithful)*

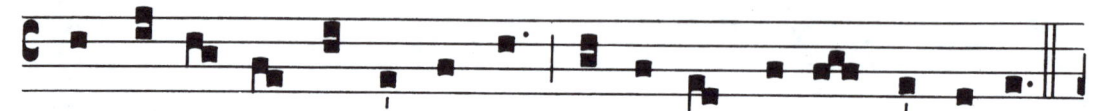

Im-ple su-pér-na grá-ti-a Quae tu cre-á-sti pé-cto-ra.
(Fill with heavenly grace) *(The hearts which Thou didst create.)*

Qui dí-ce-ris Pa-rá-cli-tus, Al-tís-si-mi dó-num De-i,
(Thou, Who art called the Paraclete,) *(Gift of the most high God,)*

Fons ví-vus, í-gnis, cá-ri-tas, Et spi-ri-tá-lis ún-cti-o. A-men.
(Fountain of life, fire, love,) *(And spiritual unction.)*

Do you remember that this neum is a *torculus* ? You will often sing it on the word *Amen*. Can you name all the neums in this hymn?

Tantum Ergo

1. Tan-tum er-go Sa-cra-mén-tum Ve-ne-ré-mur cér-nu-i:
2. Ge-ni-tó-ri, Ge-ni-tó-que Laus et ju-bi-lá-ti-o:

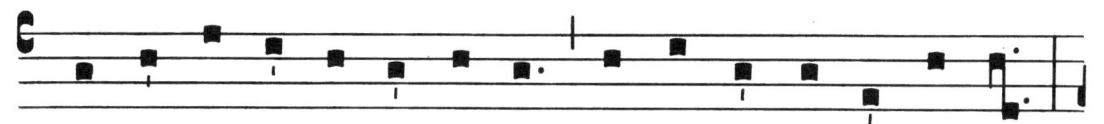

Et an-tí-quum do-cu-mén-tum No-vo cé-dat rí-tu-i:
Sá-lus, hó-nor, vír-tus quo-que Sit et be-ne-dí-cti-o:

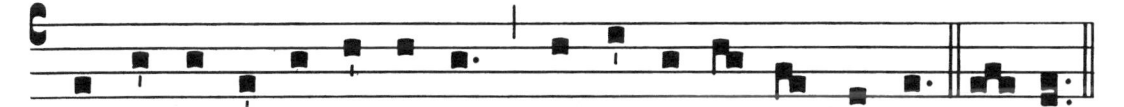

Práe-stet fí-des sup-ple-mén-tum Sén-su-um de-fé-ctu-i.
Pro-ce-dén-ti ab u-tró-que Cóm-par sit lau-dá-ti-o. A-men.

English translation for "Tantum Ergo":

Therefore, before this great Sacrament,
Let us bend low in adoration!
Let the Old Law
Give way to the New Rite.
Let faith supply
Where the senses fail!

To the Father and the Son
Praise and song of joy,
Together with salvation, honor,
Power, and blessing!
And to Him Who proceeds from Both
Equal be the praise!

Come, Spirit Blest

Translated by JOHN DRYDEN

THOMAS TALLIS

1. Come, Spir-it blest, Cre - a - tor come, from Thy bright heav'n-ly home,
2. Thou Who art called the Par - a - clete, best gift of God a - bove,
3. All glo - ry to the Fa - ther be, with His co - e - qual Son,

Come take pos-ses-sion of our souls, and make them all Thine own.
The liv-ing spring, the liv-ing fire, sweet unc-tion and true love.
The same to Thee, great Par - a - clete, while end-less a - ges run.

You will notice that *do* is on the first line when there are three flats in the key signature. *Do* is also on the first line when the key signature has four sharps.

I'm a Truck Driver

JOHN QUENTIN
CZECH FOLK TUNE

I'm a truck driv-er, as you well can see,
Traf-fic and high-ways do not wor-ry me.
I am care-ful when I drive, folks like me will stay a-live,
On the road you're al-ways safe with me.

Clap the rhythm pattern of the first phrase.
What other phrase is like it?
What phrase is almost like it?

Market Song

CAROL FULLER

One swing to a measure

1. Hay la la, ho la! Oh, Donkey and I,
2. Hay la la, ho la! If no one should buy,

Trotting to market with cherries piled high,
We'll eat those cherries, my Donkey and I;

Trotting to market with cherries piled high,
We'll eat those cherries, my Donkey and I,

Hay la la, ho la! Oh, Donkey and I.
Hay la la, ho la! If no one should buy!

Mockingbird

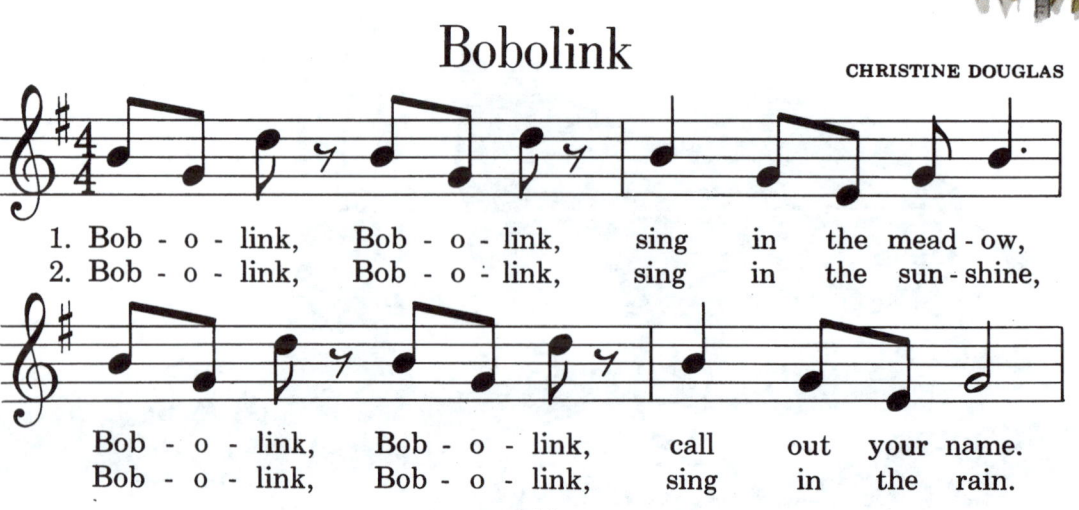

MARY WARD

1. Mock-ing-bird in the old wil-low tree,
   Sing a song with a sweet mel-o-dy,
   Oh, I nev-er could be sor-ry, and I nev-er could be sad,
   While the mock-ing-bird is a-sing-ing for me.
2. Mock-ing-bird, keep a-sing-ing your song,
   Sing it sweet, sing it all the day long,
   Oh, as long as you keep sing-ing, I'll be hap-py as can be,
   While I'm lis-ten-ing to that beau-ti-ful song.

Can you remember what the time signature in this song means?

Bobolink

CHRISTINE DOUGLAS

1. Bob-o-link, Bob-o-link, sing in the mead-ow,
   Bob-o-link, Bob-o-link, call out your name.
2. Bob-o-link, Bob-o-link, sing in the sun-shine,
   Bob-o-link, Bob-o-link, sing in the rain.

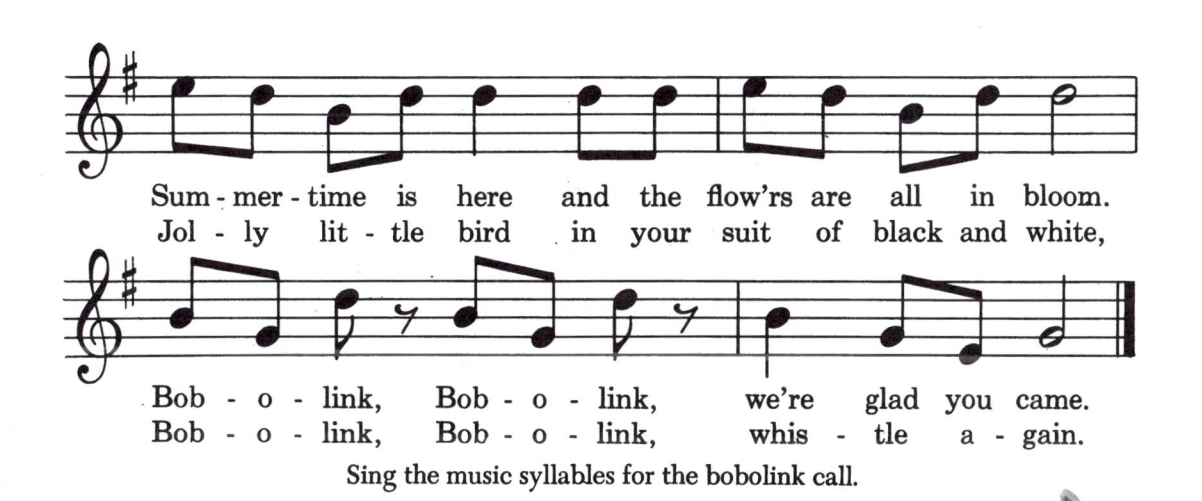

Sum - mer - time is here and the flow'rs are all in bloom.
Jol - ly lit - tle bird in your suit of black and white,

Bob - o - link, Bob - o - link, we're glad you came.
Bob - o - link, Bob - o - link, whis - tle a - gain.

Sing the music syllables for the bobolink call.

A Little Bird

English version by ROSE FYLEMAN
YUGOSLAVIAN FOLK SONG

so *do*

1. A lit - tle bird sat up - on a tree;
2. I looked at him, and he looked at me;

I looked at him, then he looked at me.
I gath - ered straw - ber - ries, one, two, three.

Be - low him there in my gar - den bed
But I have not an - y doubt, have you,

Were shin - ing straw - ber - ries ripe and red.
That lit - tle bird, he will get some too?

The key signature of four sharps tells you that *do* is on the first line.
What other key signature tells you that *do* is on the first line?

145

Hiking Song

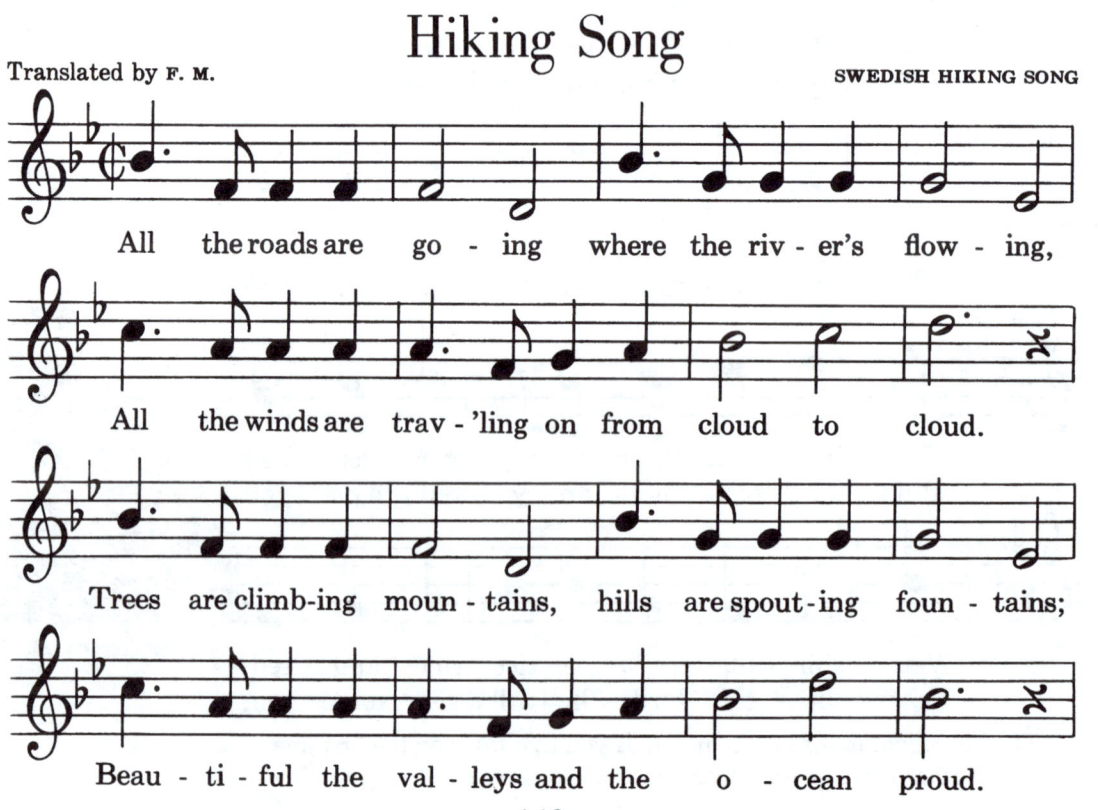

Translated by F. M.

SWEDISH HIKING SONG

All the roads are go-ing where the riv-er's flow-ing,

All the winds are trav-'ling on from cloud to cloud.

Trees are climb-ing moun-tains, hills are spout-ing foun-tains;

Beau-ti-ful the val-leys and the o-cean proud.

Come, my friends, let's fol - low wa - ter, wind and swal - low,
They are broth - ers on our way.
All our roads are go - ing where the sun is glow - ing
When we're out a - hik - ing on a hol - i - day.

In Spanish Town

MARCHETTE GAYLORD CHUTE
JAMAICAN FOLK TUNE

1. As I went walk-ing in Span - ish Town, Up and down Span - ish Town,
2. He had brought mon-keys a - cross the sea, I - vo - ry, crates of tea,
3. He said he knew of some hid - den gold In an old se - cret hold.

I met a fine sail - or so big and brown, As I went up and down.
And two lit - tle par - rots he gave to me As we went up and down.
Oh, won - der - ful, won - der - ful tales he told As we went up and down.

147

The Buffalo Head Dance

INDIAN DRUM
PLAINS INDIANS' SONG

Yay_____ yay___ wee yay yah wee yay yah hah
Go hunt the buf-fa-lo that roam on the prai-rie,

Yay_____ yay___ wee yay yah wee yay yah hah
Go hunt the buf-fa-lo that roam on the prai-rie,

Yay_____ yay___ wee yay yah wee yay yah hah
Great shag-gy buf-fa-lo that graze on the prai-rie,

Wee yay hay wee yay hay hah yah
May there be buf-fa-lo man-y,

Wee yay hay wee yay hay ah yay hah.
May there be buf-fa-lo graz-ing there.

Iroquois Song

IROQUOIS INDIAN SONG

Boys *la*

Ar - row be sure, Find the war-y deer,

Chorus

Ar - row be sure, Find the war-y deer,

Boys

Deep in the for-est dark, They are hid-ing there.

Chorus

Deep in the for-est dark, They are hid-ing there.

Play the tomtom with a rhythm of four steady notes in every measure.

Indian Dance

KATHERINE BOLT

Dance of the WARM SPRING INDIANS from OREGON

Steadily

DRUM

1. Broth-ers, let us dance;   Beat up-on the drum.
2. We will stamp our feet,   Bend our heads down low,

Make the cir-cle wid-er, wid-er! Here we come.
Lift our knees up high-er, high-er! Here we go.

Tekakwitha

CLARINE KEEHN

la la la mi

Tek-a-kwith-a, Tek-a-kwith-a, Saint-ly lit-tle In-dian maid,
Knew the riv-ers, knew the for-ests, Knew the songs the birds did sing.
Tek-a-kwith-a, Tek-a-kwith-a, Saint-ly lit-tle In-dian maid,
Loved the sun-shine, loved the flow-ers, Loved her God in ev-'ry-thing.

Pronounce *Tĕk'-a-kwĭth'-a*.

O Dandelion

UNKNOWN FINNISH FOLK TUNE

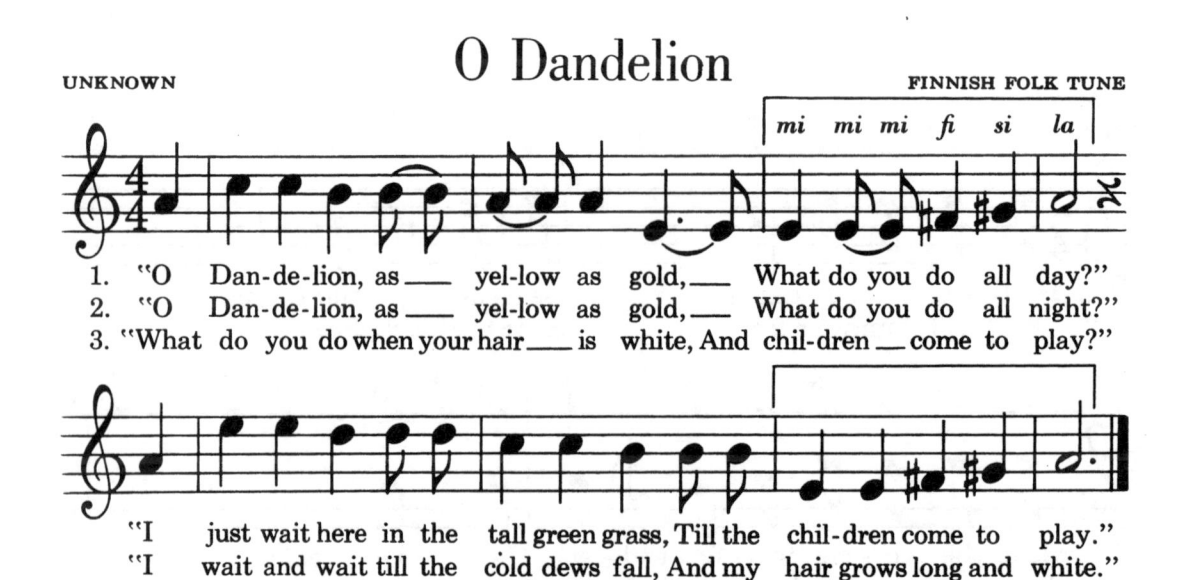

mi mi mi fi si la

1. "O Dan-de-lion, as yel-low as gold, What do you do all day?"
2. "O Dan-de-lion, as yel-low as gold, What do you do all night?"
3. "What do you do when your hair is white, And chil-dren come to play?"

"I just wait here in the tall green grass, Till the chil-dren come to play."
"I wait and wait till the cold dews fall, And my hair grows long and white."
"They take me up in their lit-tle hands, And they blow my hair a-way."

Our Lady of the Seas

MARY SYNON
DUTCH FOLK SONG

1. Blue of sky and gold of sun,
2. North-ern stars and south-ern stars,
3. Ros-y dawn and pur-ple dusk,
4. East-ern shores and west-ern shores,

Her veil is gay as these,
Her crown is bright as these,
Wild storms and gen-tle breeze,
Her love is wide as these,

She guides the sail-ors through the day,
She keeps the watch all through the night,
She guards the ships a-gainst all harm,
She brings her chil-dren safe-ly home,

Our La-dy of the Seas.
Our La-dy of the Seas.
Our La-dy of the Seas.
Our La-dy of the Seas.

The Elf

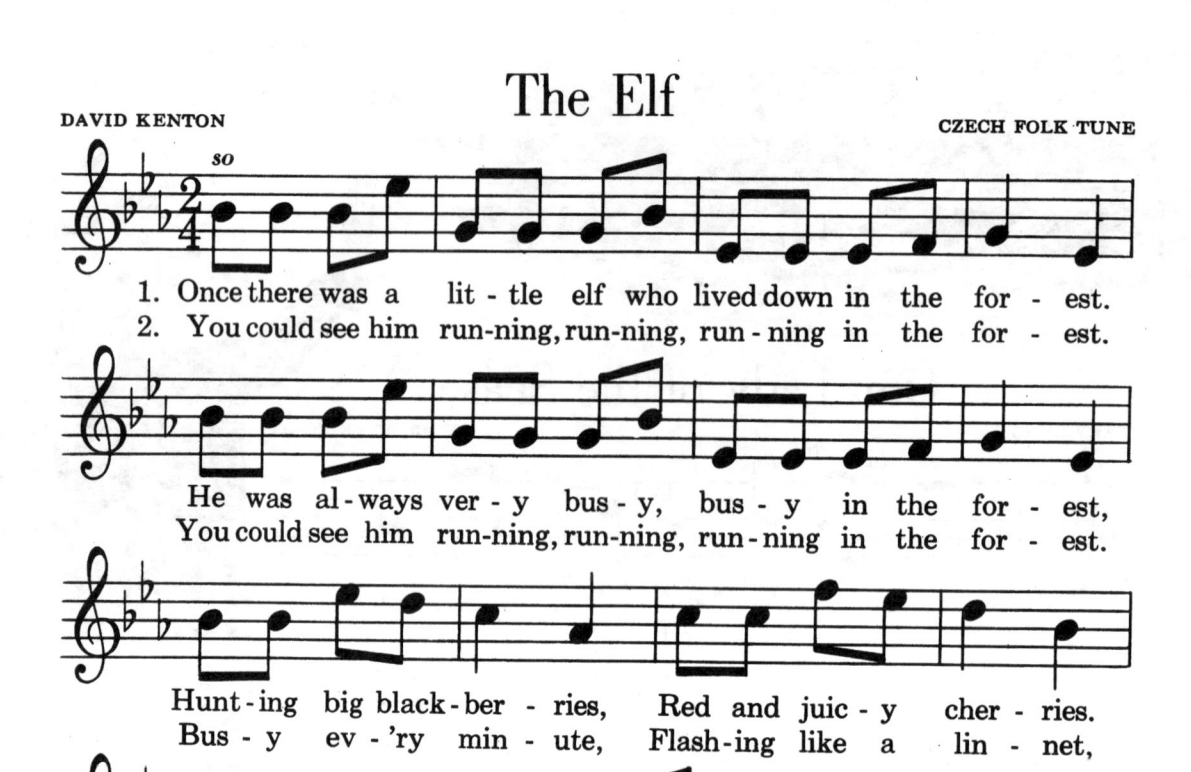

DAVID KENTON
CZECH FOLK TUNE

1. Once there was a lit-tle elf who lived down in the for-est.
2. You could see him run-ning, run-ning, run-ning in the for-est.

He was al-ways ver-y bus-y, bus-y in the for-est,
You could see him run-ning, run-ning, run-ning in the for-est.

Hunt-ing big black-ber-ries, Red and juic-y cher-ries.
Bus-y ev-'ry min-ute, Flash-ing like a lin-net,

He was ver-y bus-y, bus-y, work-ing all the day.
You could see him run-ning, run-ning, run-ning all the day.

Look at the time signature. How many beats are there in a measure? Tap them lightly as you sing.

A Magic Fern

After the original by LOUISE KESSLER
ESTONIAN FOLK SONG

1. In the woods there is a mag-ic fern, Mag-ic fern, mag-ic fern,
2. Find the mag-ic flow-er 'neath the moon, 'Neath the moon, 'neath the moon,

In the woods there is a mag-ic fern, Bloom-ing in the soft moon-light.
Find the mag-ic flow-er 'neath the moon, Find-ing it will bring good luck.

Come, come, fol - low me, Danc - ing through the woods with glee!
Come, come, dance and sing! In the woods our voic - es ring.

Come, come, fol - low me! Soon the mag - ic fern we'll see.
Come, come, dance and sing! Joy to me the fern will bring.

Find all the measures that are alike.

The Mouser

Translated by FRANCES FORD

AUSTRIAN FOLK SONG

1. The cat comes creep - ing by, take care, take care,
2. The cat has gone a - way, a - way, a - way,

With green and greed - y eye. Be - ware! Be - ware!
He caught no mouse to - day, to - day, to - day!

The lit - tle mice go scam - p'ring when they hear his vel - vet paws,
The lit - tle mice come skip - ping from their se - cret hid - ing holes,

They fear his cru - el claws.
Their se - cret hid - ing holes.

Here is another song with four flats.
Do you remember where to find *do*?

153

Susan Blue

KATE GREENAWAY
FRANCIS HILLIARD

First group. (Voices, violins, flutes and melody instruments.)

Oh, Su-san Blue, How do you do?

Second group. (Voices, violins, flutes and melody instruments.)

Oh, Su-san Blue, How do you

Please may I go for a walk with you?

do? Please may I go for a walk with

Where shall we go? Oh, yes I know,

you? Where shall we go? Oh, yes I

Down in the mead-ow where cow-slips grow.
know, Down in the mead-ow where cow-slips grow.

Hush, Little Baby

TRADITIONAL

1. Hush, lit-tle ba-by, don't say a word,
2. If that diamond ring turns brass,
3. If that bil-ly goat gets bon-y,

Pa-pa's goin' to buy you a mock-ing-bird,
Pa-pa's goin' to buy you a look-ing glass.
Pa-pa's goin' to buy you a Shet-land po-ny.

If that mock-ing bird don't sing,
If that look-ing glass gets broke,
If that po-ny runs a-way,

Pa-pa's goin' to buy you a dia-mond ring.
Pa-pa's goin' to buy you a bil-ly goat.
Pa-pa's goin' to buy you an-oth-er some day.

There Was a Little French Girl
La Bergère

FRENCH FOLK SONG

There was a lit - tle French girl,
Il é - tait un' ber - gè - re

Oh, ron ron ron, pe - tit pa - ta - pon.
Et ron ron ron, pe - tit pa - ta - pon.

There was a lit - tle French girl
Il é - tait un' ber - gè - re

Who watched her snow - white sheep, ron ron,
Qui gar - dait ses mou - tons, ron ron,

Who watched her snow - white sheep._____
Qui gar - dait ses mou - tons._____

You will enjoy singing this song in French.

Little Lonely Shepherd

Paraphrased from the FRENCH

FRENCH BERGERETTE

1. Poor lit - tle lone - ly shep - herd, What do you do all the day?

156

Play us a sweet lit - tle bal - lad, Play us a lit - tle lay.¹

What do you do in the morn - ing? At night when the sun has set?

Poor lit - tle lone - ly shep - herd, Play for us on your mu - sette.²

¹A *lay* is a simple song. ²A *musette* is a small bagpipe with a sweet tone. It was popular in France in the 18th century. Pronounce *moo-sĕt'*.

The Echo

ABIGAIL COFFIN
WILL EARHART

The ech - o is call - ing, call - ing,

The ech - o is call - ing, call - ing,

Call - ing back to me, to me.

Sing the echo softly each time.
The sign ⌒ means to hold a note longer. It is called a *fermata*.

157

Old Dan Tucker

DAN EMMETT TRADITIONAL

1. I went to town the oth-er night,
2. Old Dan Tuck-er was a might-y man;

I heard the noise, then saw the fight,
He washed his face in a fry-ing pan,

The watch-man was a-run-ning 'round
He combed his hair with a wag-on wheel,

Cry-ing, "Old Dan Tuck-er's come to town!"
And he died with a tooth-ache in his heel.

Chorus

So get out the way, Old Dan Tuck-er,

You're too late to stay for sup-per,

158

Sup - per's o - ver, break - fast's cook - ing,

Old Dan Tuck - er stand - ing look - ing!

Bedtime

L. MITCHELL THORNTON
SISTER JOHN JOSEPH, C.S.J.

mi la
I'm sleep - y in the morn - ing when the mill wheel croons

la la so so
A lull - a, lull - a, lull - a - by of drow - sy tunes.

I'm sleep - y in the gar - den when the sun is shin - ing bright,

But I'm nev - er, nev - er sleep - y when it's bed - time at night.

159

I Asked My Mother for Fifty Cents

OLD RHYME   **JOHN REGIS FETE**

I asked my mother for fifty cents
To see the el-e-phant jump the fence.
He jumped so high, he touched the sky,
And nev-er came back till the Fourth of Ju-ly,
So high,_____ so high,_____
He nev-er came back till the Fourth of Ju-ly.

Sing, Sing Together

ROUND

1. Sing, sing to-geth-er, mer-ri-ly, mer-ri-ly sing;
2. Sing, sing to-geth-er, mer-ri-ly, mer-ri-ly sing;
3. Sing, sing, sing, sing.

Rosa

TRANSLATED FLEMISH FOLK SONG

1. Ro-sa, let us be danc-ing, be danc-ing, be danc-ing,
2. Come, now let us be danc-ing, be danc-ing, be danc-ing,

Ro-sa, let us be danc-ing, be danc-ing, dear. *Fine*
Come now, let us be danc-ing, be danc-ing here.

Ro-sa laughed so mer-ri-ly, Tossed her head so sau-ci-ly,

D.C. al Fine

"I'll dance with you,"

D.C. al Fine means to go back to the beginning of the song and sing to *Fine*, which means *the end*.

Picnic Day

CARLA MARIA BIANCHI
SCOTTISH FOLK TUNE

1. Bring your bat and bring your ball, Bring your catch-er's mitt and all.
2. We can row a-cross the lake. There's a boat that we can take.

Hur-ry, hur-ry when we call, For it is our pic-nic day.
What a jol-ly crew we make, For it is our pic-nic day.

Sand-wich-es and cook-ies too, Some for me and some for you.
Ice-cream cones and can-dy too, Some for me and some for you.

Hur-ry Jim and Jane and Sue For it is our pic-nic day.
Hur-ry Jack and Joe and Lou For it is our pic-nic day.

What does the *fermata* tell you to do?

The Star-Spangled Banner

FRANCIS SCOTT KEY
JOHN STAFFORD SMITH

1. Oh, ___ say! can you see, ___ by the dawn's ear-ly light,
2. Oh, ___ thus be it ev-er when ___ free-men shall stand

162

What so proud-ly we hailed at the twi-light's last gleam-ing,
Be - tween their loved homes and the war's des - o - la - tion!
Whose broad stripes and bright stars, through the per - il - ous fight,
Blest with vic - t'ry and peace, may the heav'n-res - cued land
O'er the ram-parts we watched were so gal - lant - ly stream-ing?
Praise the Pow'r that hath made and pre-served us a na - tion!
And the rock - ets' red glare, the bombs burst - ing in air,
Then con - quer we must, when our cause it is just,
Gave proof through the night that our flag was still there.
And this be our mot - to: "In God is our trust!"
Oh, say does that Star-Span-gled Ban - ner yet wave
And the Star-Span-gled Ban - ner in tri - umph shall wave
O'er the land of the free and the home of the brave?
O'er the land of the free and the home of the brave!

Father Juniper and The Bells of Capistrano

Narrator. Father Juniper walked slowly along the sandy beach of California. On one side the mountains rose high to a bright blue sky; on the other side the Pacific Ocean sparkled in the sunshine. Sea gulls wheeled and circled over the head of the padre as he walked along. They seemed to be curious about this man who plodded along in the sand and looked across the ocean toward the horizon.

Father Juniper wore a coarse, brown robe; on his bare feet were rough leather sandals, so shabby and worn that even the poorest Indian would not want them. But Father Juniper cared not at all about his patched clothes or his worn sandals. He was a Spanish Franciscan who had come to California to save the souls of the Indians. He was praying for them as he walked beside the beautiful Pacific.

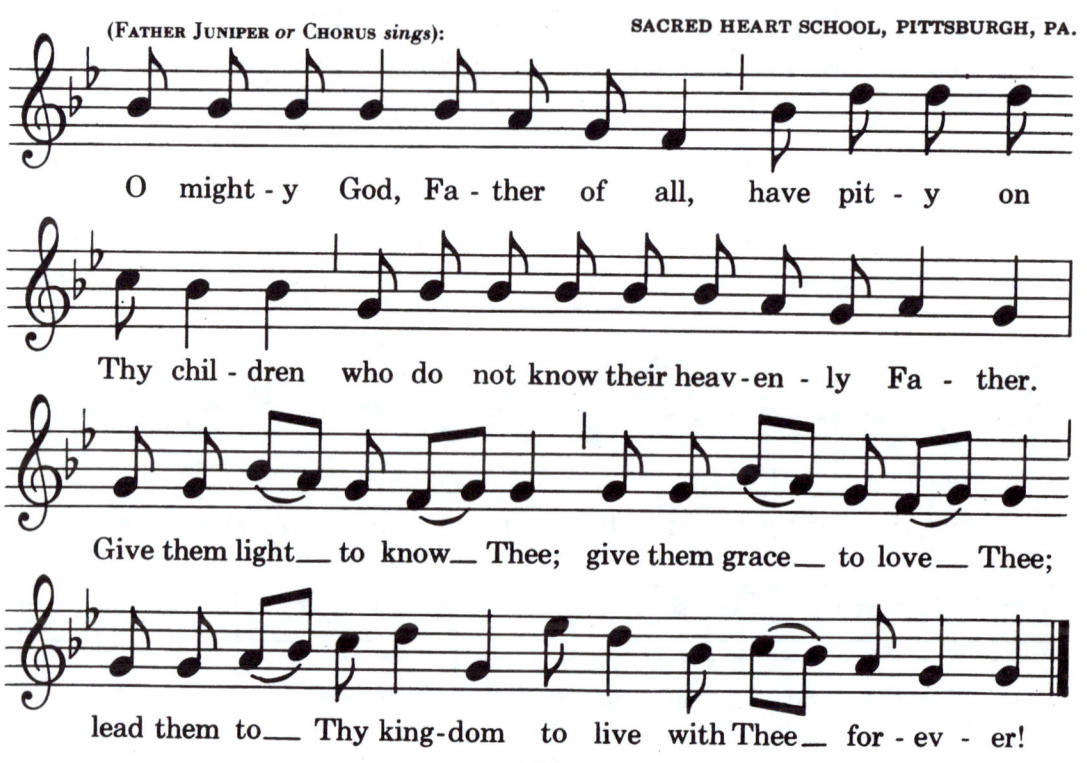

(FATHER JUNIPER or CHORUS sings):   SACRED HEART SCHOOL, PITTSBURGH, PA.

O might-y God, Fa-ther of all, have pit-y on Thy chil-dren who do not know their heav-en-ly Fa-ther. Give them light to know Thee; give them grace to love Thee; lead them to Thy king-dom to live with Thee for-ev-er!

Verse Speaking Choir:
>Father in heaven, bless my hands
>That I may serve Thy children.
>Father in heaven, bless my tongue
>That I may teach Thy children.
>Father in heaven, bless my heart
>That I may love Thy children;
>That I may love Thee, heavenly Father,
>Now and forever. Amen.

Narrator. Again and again Father Juniper looked out toward the horizon. He was watching for a sail, for the flash of white in the distance that would tell him the ships had come from Mexico. For many long weeks he had waited for the ships. They carried a precious cargo—food and clothing for the Indians; seeds, vines, and fruit trees for the mission; letters, perhaps, from Spain and Mexico. Best of all, they would bring the mission bells, the bells that would call the people to Holy Mass.

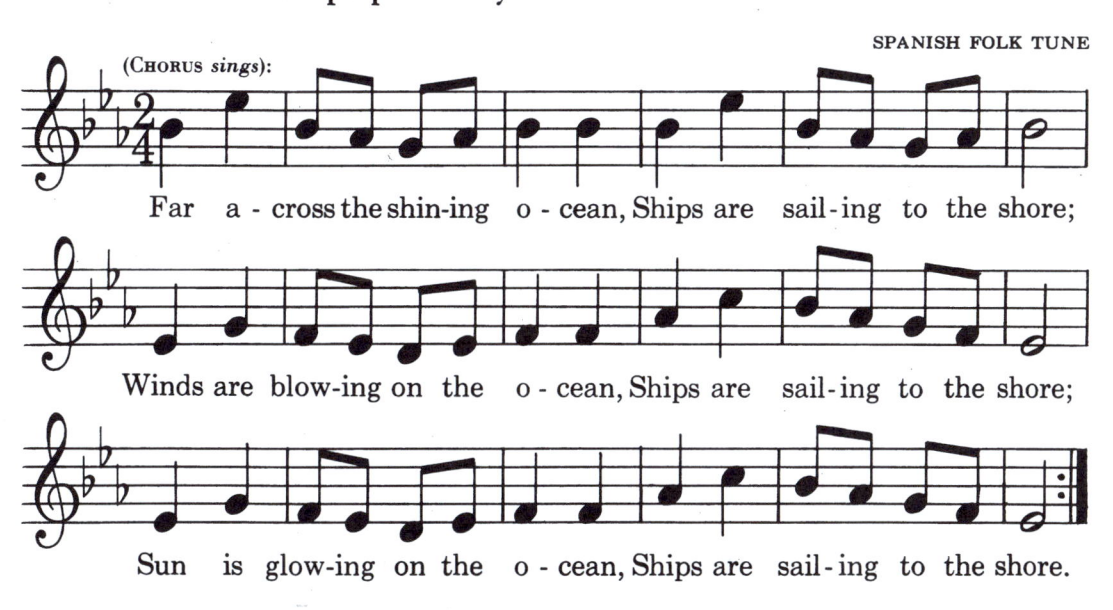

SPANISH FOLK TUNE

(CHORUS *sings*):

Far across the shining ocean, Ships are sailing to the shore;

Winds are blowing on the ocean, Ships are sailing to the shore;

Sun is glowing on the ocean, Ships are sailing to the shore.

Narrator. In the hills, at the foot of the mountain, the new mission church was slowly rising toward the sky. Soon it would be finished; and when the bells came and were hung in the belfry, the Indians would come to hear the word of God and to be baptized. Father Juniper prayed that many would come and be converted. He placed his confidence in Mary, Queen of Heaven, that this new mission of San Juan Capistrano would be blessed with many converts. Standing there beside the Pacific he sang a hymn to her:

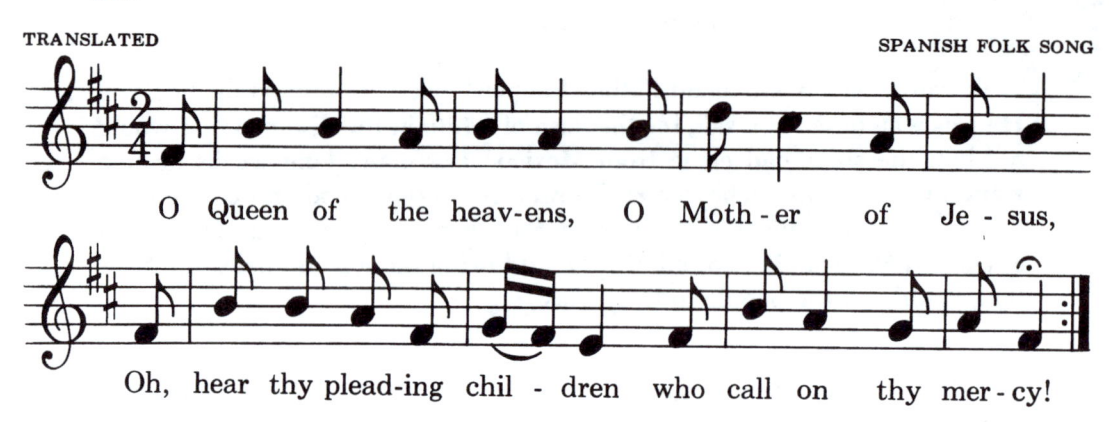

TRANSLATED   **SPANISH FOLK SONG**

O Queen of the heav-ens, O Moth-er of Je-sus,
Oh, hear thy plead-ing chil-dren who call on thy mer-cy!

Narrator. At last Father Juniper saw a gleam of white far out on the ocean. A ship! Yes, it was really there! The ships had come from Mexico. The bells of San Juan Capistrano would soon be ringing.

(CHORUS):

Soon the bells will be ring-ing, bless-ed bells sweet-ly ring-ing,

"Bless the Lord, sing His prais-es now and ev-er-more."

Verse Speaking Choir:
At morn, and noon, and evening,
The mission bells will ring;
The mountains and the ocean
Will hear them echoing.
Ring out, sweet bells,
Ring loud, sweet bells,
Call everyone to prayer.

Narrator. When the ships came to anchor they were quickly unloaded. The precious bells were carried up the hill to the church that was nearly finished. They were beautiful bells, four of them. Father Juniper tapped them lightly just to hear their beautiful tone.

(*Play the bells softly.*)

Verse Speaking Choir:

So high the mighty mountains, So clear the silver ringing
So wide the shining ocean, Of bells in rhythm swinging;
So warm the winds that blow The winds will bear their message
Across the sea and mountain. Across the land and sea.

Narrator. Everyone worked hard to finish the church and the belfry. One day a messenger came galloping up the hill. The men stopped working on the church and gathered around to hear the news. It was very bad news. Unfriendly Indians had attacked the mission of San Diego. They had killed the padre and burned the church. The people of San Diego begged Father Juniper to come to help them, and Father Juniper knew he must go. All the work on San Juan Capistrano would have to stop until he returned. The beautiful bells were buried deep in the earth where they would be safe, and Father Juniper rode away to San Diego. As his mule jogged along the road he prayed to Our Lady and St. Francis that he might soon return to San Juan Capistrano.

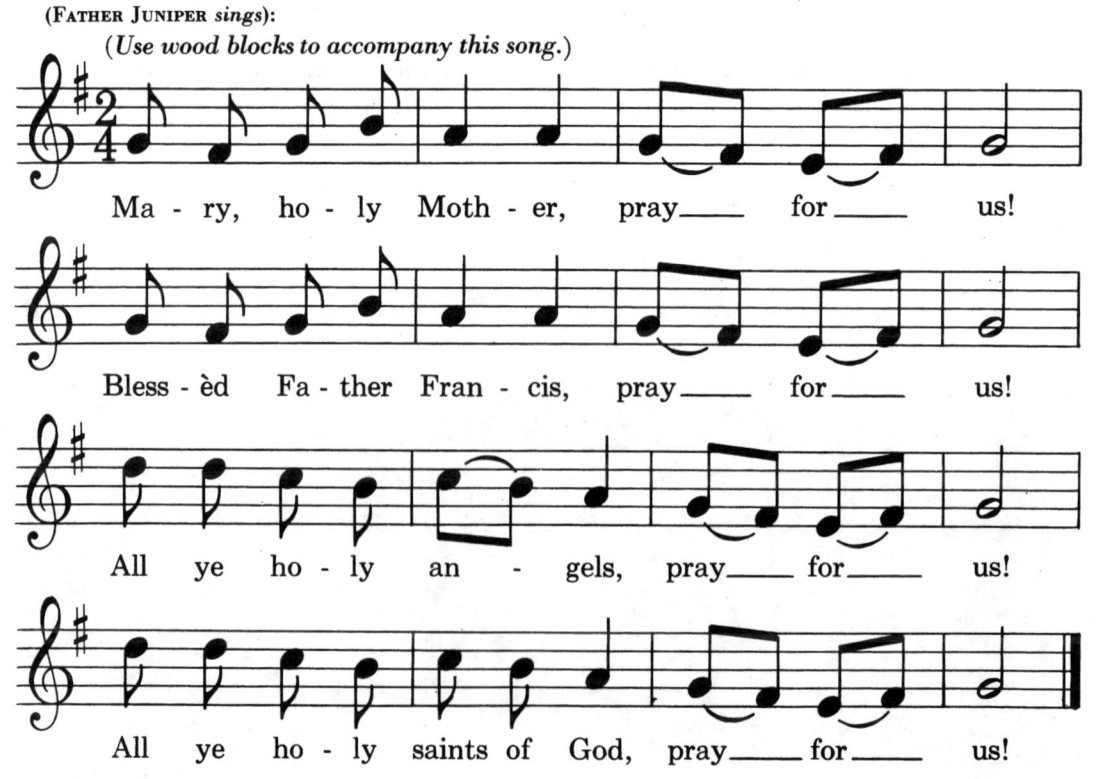

(FATHER JUNIPER *sings*):
(*Use wood blocks to accompany this song.*)

Ma - ry, ho - ly Moth - er, pray___ for___ us!

Bless - èd Fa - ther Fran - cis, pray___ for___ us!

All ye ho - ly an - gels, pray___ for___ us!

All ye ho - ly saints of God, pray___ for___ us!

Narrator. Sometimes as they rode along, Father Juniper and his men would pray the Rosary.

Verse Speaking Choir. **Hail, Mary, full of grace, the Lord is with thee. Blessèd art thou among women, and blessèd is the fruit of thy womb, Jesus.**

(Father Juniper and Chorus sing):

Ho - ly Ma - ry, Moth - er of God, pray for us sin - ners, now and at the hour of our death. A - men.

Narrator. Several years passed and still Father Juniper was far from his mission; still the bells lay buried beside the blue Pacific. Sometimes Father Juniper would imagine he heard them calling him. Then he would pray to Our Lady and St. Francis that soon he might ride back to San Juan Capistrano.

(*Play the bells very softly while the verse speaking choir recites.*)

Verse Speaking Choir: **Holy Mother, Mary, Blessèd Father Francis, All ye holy angels hasten my returning.**

Narrator. **And then one day friendly Indians saw a mule train on the road to Capistrano. It came slowly, for the mules were heavily burdened. Soldiers rode ahead on fine Spanish horses. One of the mules carried on his back a man in a patched brown robe. Father Juniper was returning to San Juan Capistrano! His heart was full of great joy, for in the mule packs there were vestments and holy vessels for the church, seeds and vines and fruit trees for the mission. And the bells were still waiting, buried safely deep in the earth.**

(CHORUS *sings*):
WOOD BLOCKS

Down the hill comes a train of mules with heav-y bur-dens,

See them go slow-ly on the road to Ca-pis-tra-no.

Gold-en sun shin-ing on the blue and smil-ing o-cean.

Show the way, guide them on the road to Ca-pis-tra-no.

Narrator. Now everyone went to work to finish the mission church. The soldiers and Indians helped, and Father Juniper seemed to do more work than all the rest together. The walls went up and up and soon the church was finished. The buried bells were dug up from their hiding place and hung high in the belfry. Next morning when the sun rose above the mountains, the bells of Capistrano rang the Angelus. And as Father Juniper knelt to pray, his heart was filled with great joy, for the bells were ringing out over ocean and mountains the glad story of our Redemption, the story that begins with the words of the Angel Gabriel:

Verse Speaking Choir. (One Voice) Hail, Mary, full of grace, the Lord is with thee. Blessèd art thou among women, and blessèd is the fruit of thy womb, Jesus.
(All) Holy Mary, Mother of God, pray for us sinners now and at the hour of our death. Amen.

SPANISH FOLK TUNE

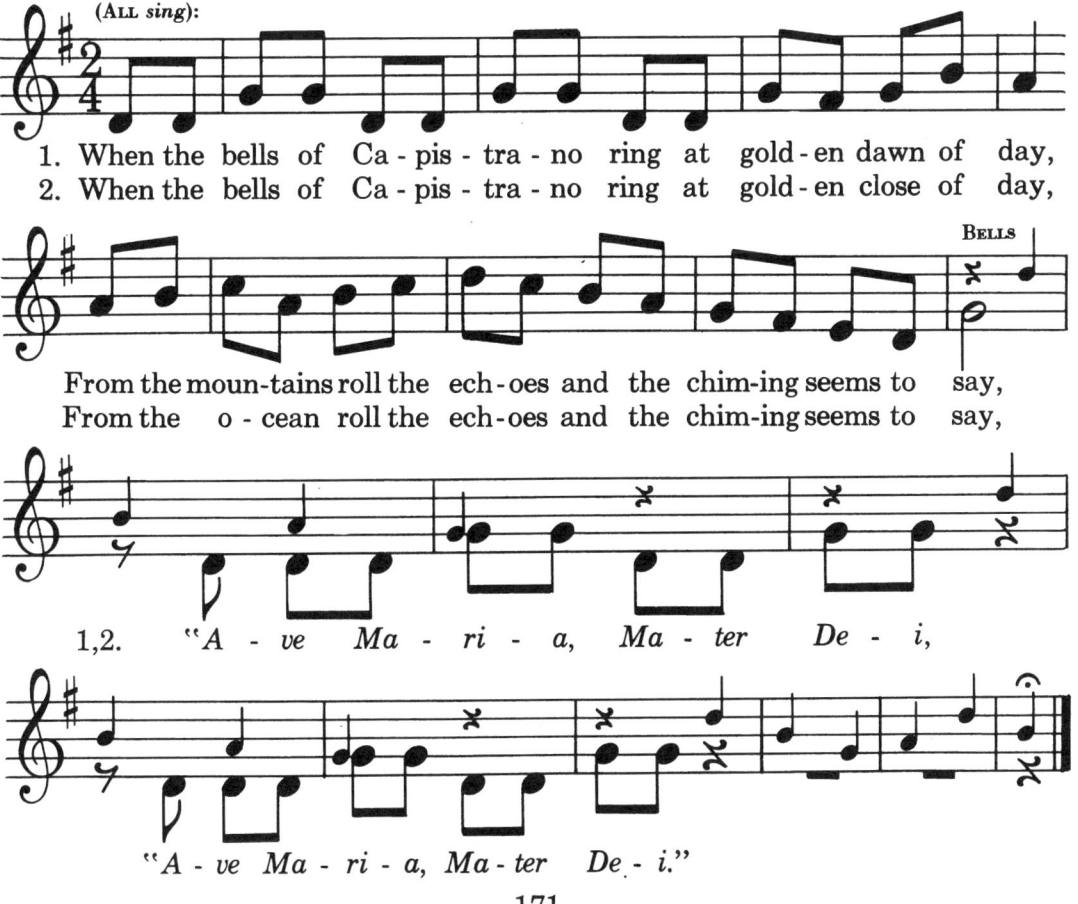

(ALL *sing*):

1. When the bells of Ca - pis - tra - no ring at gold-en dawn of day,
2. When the bells of Ca - pis - tra - no ring at gold-en close of day,

From the moun-tains roll the ech-oes and the chim-ing seems to say,
From the o - cean roll the ech-oes and the chim-ing seems to say,

1,2. "A - ve Ma - ri - a, Ma - ter De - i,

"A - ve Ma - ri - a, Ma - ter De - i."

We Sing the Mass

Kyrie

MASS XVI

Ký - ri - e e - lé - i - son. *iij* Chrí - ste e - lé - i - son. *iij*

Ký - ri - e e - lé - i - son. *ij.* Ký - ri - e e - lé - i - son.

Gloria

MASS XV

Priest sings: Gló - ri - a in ex - cél - sis Dé - o. **Choir:** Et in tér - ra pax ho - mí - ni - bus

bó - nae vo - lun - tá - tis. Lau - dá - mus te. Be - ne - dí - ci - mus te.

A - do - rá - mus te. Glo - ri - fi - cá - mus te.

Grá - ti - as á - gi - mus ti - bi pro - pter má - gnam gló - ri - am tú - am.

Dó - mi - ne Dé - us, Rex cae - lé - stis, Dé - us Pá - ter o - mní - po - tens.

172

Alphabetical Index

[Recorded songs in Albums 4–A cms and 4–B cms are indicated after the song titles.]

Adeste Fideles, 62
Advent Wreath, The, 48 (4–A)
Agnus Dei, 36
Agnus Dei (Chant notation), 36
All the Birds Will Soon Be Here, 128 (4–B)
All Through the Night, 29 (4–B)
Alleluia, 120
America, 24
Annunciation, The, 112 (4–A)
At Easter Time, 121 (4–A)
Autumn Leaves, 18

Bedtime, 159
Bell Ringer, The, 139
Bless the Lord, 45 (4–A)
Bobolink, 144
Brother, Come and Dance, 53
Brown Bird, The, 129 (4–A)
Buffalo Head Dance, The, 148 (4–A)
Bumblebee, The, 128
Busy Tailors, The, 109 (4–A)
Bye, Baby, Bye, 55 (4–B)

Canticle of Praise, 44 (4–A)
Child Is Born in Bethlehem, A, 66 (4–A)
Christmas Blessings, 68 (4–A)
Christmas Is Coming, 57 (4–B)
Christmas Song, A, 64
Christus Vincit, 36
Columbus and the Sailors, 19
Come, Spirit Blest, 141
Come to the Manger, 70
Country Dance, 101 (4–A)

Dancing Long Ago, 27 (4–A)
Down in the Valley, 115
Drummer Boy, The, 37

Echo, The, 157
Elf, The, 152
Evening Hymn, 89 (4–A)
Evening Prayer, 28

Falling Snow, 99 (4–A)
Father Juniper and the Bells of Capistrano (Play), 164

Forgive Us Our Sins, O Lord, 113
Four in a Boat, 126
Four Winds, The, 131
Fox and Goose, 17
Friendly Beasts, The, 67

Gently the Snow Is Falling, 90 (4–B)
Geography Travels, 30
Gloria Patri, 28 (4–A)
Go to Sleep, My Baby, 40 (4–A)
Golden Slumbers, 41
Grasshopper Green, 10
Great God of Love, 7 (4–A)
Greedy Ducks, 123

Haul Away, Joe, 93
Have You Ever Seen the Daisies? 127 (4–B)
Haydn, Franz Joseph: Biographical Sketch, 100
Heavens Are Telling, The, 102
Here Lies a Baby, 71
Hickory, Dickory Dock, 138
Hiking Song, 146 (4–A)
Holy Mary, Blessèd Mary, 8
Holy Mother, 32
Home on the Range, 134
Hungarian Dance, 137
Hunters, The, 52
Hush, Little Baby, 155 (4–A)
Hymn of Praise, 121

I Am the Wind, 106 (4–B)
I Asked My Mother for Fifty Cents, 160
I Listen to the Whistles, 8
If I Had a Nickel, 50
I'm a Truck Driver, 142
I'm Glad, 107
I'm the Doctor Eisenbart, 108 (4–A)
In October, 24
In Spanish Town, 147 (4–A)
Indian Dance, 149
Indian Lullaby, 132
Indian Summer Days, 19
Iroquois Song, 149

Jack O'Lantern, 34
Jay Birds, The, 50

Jesu dulcis memoria, 88 (4–B)
Jesus, Tender Shepherd, Hear Me, 133
Jingle Bells, 58
Joseph, Our Protector, 104

Kyrie Eleison, 104

Land of the Dutch, Dutch, Dutch, The, 124
Little Bird, A, 145
Little Brown Brother, 132
Little Lonely Shepherd, 156
Little Squirrel, A, 18
Little Willie, 22
'Liza Jane, 118
Lovely Infant, 66 (4–A)
Lullaby to the Infant Jesus, 72 (4–A)

Magic Fern, A, 152
Maiden Mother Meek and Mild, 32
Maiden Mother Meek and Mild (Chant notation), 33
Market Song, 143
Mary's Child Was Jesus, 69
Master Weaver, The, 35
Mockingbird, 144 (4–A)
Morning Hymn, 89
Morning Song, 31
Mother Moon, The, 127
Mother of Christ, 113
Mouser, The, 153 (4–A)
Music, 14
My Cricket, 110
My Home's in Montana, 38

New Created World, A, 102
New Year, 84
Night Herding Song, 39 (4–A)
Nine Red Horsemen, 26 (4–A)

O Come, O Come, Emmanuel, 46
O Dandelion, 150
O Filii et Filiae, 120 (4–A)
O Jesus, Lord, Thy Holy Name, 88 (4–B)
O Land So Beautiful, 25
O Salutaris, 60
Old Dan Tucker, 158 (4–A)
Old Folks at Home, 116
Old Man Thunder, 130
On the Road to Damascus, 91
Our Country, 96
Our Lady of the Seas, 151 (4–A)

Our Lady's Children, 94
Our Lady's Lullaby, 94
Our School Bus, 13

Parce Domine, 103
Pawpaw Patch, The, 119
Pedro and the Goats, 42 (4–A)
Picnic Day, 162
Polka, The, 16 (4–A)
Prayer for a Little Child, 91
Protect Us, O Lord, 60 (4–A)

Rain, The, 9
Rainbow, The, 131
Reuben and Rachel, 85
Ring, Ring the Banjo! 117
River, The, 114 (4–B)
Robin Hood and Little John, 111 (4–B)
Rosa, 161

Saint Joseph's Song, 105 (4–A)
Saint Peter, 90
Salve Mater, 33
Sanctus—Benedictus, 61
Schooner Sally, The, 92 (4–B)
Seek Ye the Lord, 45
Seven Frogs, 110
Silent Night, 65 (4–B)
Sing, Sing Together, 161
Skaters, The, 86
Snow, The, 54 (4–A)
Song before Christmas, 56
Soon Will the Christ Child Come, 47
Spring Music, 125
Stabat Mater, 103
Star-Spangled Banner, The, 162 (4–B)
Step Softly, Little Donkey, 83 (4–A)
Stories of Travel, 59
Sung at Harvest Time, 43 (4–B)
Susan Blue, 154
Swan Boats, The, 12

Tantum Ergo, 140
Taps, 37
Tekakwitha, 150
Thanks to Our God, 100
Thanksgiving Song, 44
There Was a Little French Girl, 156 (4–B)
There Was a Little Ship, 106
Three Little Chickens, 122
Three Kings, The (Play), 74

Three Ponies, 51
To Christ the King, 28 (4-A)
Tree, The, 114
Two Little Clouds, 15

Under the Snow, 98
Up Yonder, 136

Valentine Surprise, A, 95
Veni Creator Spiritus, 140 (4-A)

We Built a Snowman in the Yard, 92
We Sing the Mass, 20
We Sing the Mass, 172 (4-A)
While the Balalaikas Play, 135
Wind and Rain, 23
Wind, The, 15
Windmill, 11

Yankee Doodle, 97